LETTERS FROM THE
HEART OF GOD

D0196113

LETTERS FROM THE
HEART OF GOD

Clift & Kathleen
RICHARDS

VICTORY HOUSE
Tulsa, Oklahoma

Letters From the Heart of God

Copyright © 2002 by F. Clift and Kathleen Richards

ISBN: 0-932081-76-2

Published by Victory House, Inc.

P.O. Box 700238

Tulsa, Oklahoma 74170

(918) 747-5009

Acknowledgments

The authors wish to thank their editor, Lloyd Hildebrand, and the staff at Victory House for their invaluable assistance, help, and guidance in the process of writing this book.

Contents

Introduction

A few years ago we were ministering in a large church in Georgia. While there we enjoyed wonderful fellowship with the members of the congregation and the pastor and his family. The pastor's son, a boy of six or so, called his father "papa," and his use of this special term of endearment and honor caused us to recall a word that appears only three times in the New Testament—"Abba."

This Aramaic/Syro-Chaldaic word is borrowed from the language of childhood, and it literally means "Papa." It is used to show strong affection, intimacy, and deep respect for one's father.

On the night before His betrayal, while praying in the Garden of Gethsemane, Jesus cried out, "Abba, Father, all things are possible for You. Take this cup away from Me; nevertheless, not what I will, but what You will" (Mark 14:36, NKJV).

Jesus lived in glorious intimacy with His heavenly Father, and this led Him to address God as Abba—"Papa." This same term of endearment, Paul points out, is one the Holy Spirit places in the hearts of all believers because of God's desire for greater intimacy with them. (See Rom. 8:15 and Gal. 4:6.)

The more we looked into the concept of intimacy with God, based on the word Abba, the more we grew convinced that there was a need for a book that would draw God's children into a close personal relationship with their heavenly Father. This led us to write *Knowing God Intimately* in 2001, as God began to reveal himself as Abba to us. Thus, an exciting journey of ongoing spiritual discovery continued to unfold.

Letters From the Heart of God is an outgrowth of this joyous adventure. We began to wonder what it would be like to receive personal letters from our God in heaven. What would He say to us? What themes would He stress? What tone would His letters convey?

We turned to the Bible, as we asked the Holy Spirit to guide us in the writing of this book, for the Bible itself is a letter from the heart of God, which Paul says is ". . .profitable for doctrine, for reproof, for correction, for instruction in righteousness, that the man of God may be complete, thoroughly equipped for every good work" (2 Tim. 3:16).

The self-revealing God of the Bible began to speak to our hearts from His heart, and He led us each step of the way in the writing of *Letters From the Heart of God*. We learned that He keeps on revealing himself to us—as our

Abba—through our Lord and Savior Jesus Christ.

Jesus said, "I am the door" (John 10:9), and as we go through Him, a deep intimacy with our Abba-God develops.

Thomas asked Jesus, "Lord, we do not know where You are going, and how can we know the way?" (John 14:5, NKJV). Jesus gave him a simple and direct answer: "I am the way, the truth, and the life. No one comes to the Father except through Me" (John 14:6, NKJV).

Soon thereafter, Philip said to Jesus, "Lord, show us the Father, and it is sufficient for us" (John 14:8, NKJV). Jesus responded with a mild rebuke, "Have I been with you so long, and yet you have not known Me, Philip? He who has seen Me has seen the Father; so how can you say, 'Show us the Father'?" (John 14:9, NKJV).

God has chosen to reveal himself to us through His Son, Jesus Christ, who is "The Word made flesh" (John 1:14). Because we are in Christ, therefore, we are able to enjoy intimate fellowship with Abba Father, and it was for this purpose that God created us.

During the reign of terror imposed upon Cambodians by the Khmer Rouge, the story was told of a group of villagers encircled by soldiers who were threatening to kill them.

The people were ordered to fall on the ground with their faces in the dirt. This group of peasants obeyed their Khmer Rouge persecutors immediately, for they were literally surrounded by these terrifying men who were aiming their rifles directly at them.

One person began to pray to a particular deity, and several others followed suit, praying to various deities of their religion. In the midst of this chanting, one villager cried out, "Pray to the God who hung on a cross!" This believer was pointing the people to Jesus, God's Son, and the desperate crowd immediately began to call upon Him. This unusual prayer meeting went on for a few minutes, until one man looked up from the ground. The soldiers were gone! Then, the whole village rejoiced with tears of joy and gratitude. As you might expect, many of them became Christians that very day.

Jesus revealed His all-powerful Father to them, and through Him each one of us is able to draw close to Abba—our loving Papa. The Bible says, "Draw near to God, and He will draw near to you" (James 4:8, NKJV).

Letters From the Heart of God will help you draw near to God. It is a book filled with God's love, wisdom, will, and blessing. The uplifting letters in this book will bring you closer to God through the faith-building practice of meditating upon the Scriptures, which were inspired by our heavenly Father, who loves you with an everlasting love.

Each of the topical letters discloses the Father's plans and purposes for you, as they are based entirely upon His Word—the holy Bible. The personal flavor of the letters makes it seem as if God is writing to you—even speaking to you, His special child—specifically, personally, and individually. These inspiring letters are compiled from various Bible references, which are footnoted with superscript numerals in the text and listed at the end of each letter.

As you read, let God speak to your heart. The result will be a greater intimacy with your heavenly Father than you ever thought possible. This is what He promises, "For I know the thoughts that I think toward you. . . thoughts of peace and not of evil, to give you a future and a hope. Then you will call upon Me and go and pray to Me, and I will listen to you. And you will seek Me and find Me, when you search for Me with all your heart" (Jer. 29:11-13, NKJV).

GOD IS YOUR LOVING FATHER

Yet for us there is one God, the Father; of whom are
all things, and we for Him; and one Lord Jesus Christ,
through whom are all things,
and through whom we live.
(1 Cor. 8:6, NKJV)

God Is Faithful to You

God, your Father, is absolutely faithful to every word He speaks. The Bible is His Word to you, and it is filled with your Father's special promises to you. These promises are personally addressed to you, for you are a beloved child of your heavenly Father. As His child, you are member of the family of God and a joint heir with Jesus Christ.

Paul wrote, "The Spirit Himself bears witness with our spirit that we are children of God, and if children, then heirs—heirs of God and joint heirs with Christ" (Rom. 8:16-17, NKJV).

Don't these realizations fill your heart with wonder and gratitude? Don't they make you want to cry out, "Thank you, Father!"? The great Creator of heaven and earth has made you His own child, and He wants to give you every good and perfect gift. (See James 1:17.) But this is not all the inheritance entails.

Your Father wants you to increase in your knowledge of Him, " .strengthened with all might, according to His glorious power, for all patience and longsuffering with joy; giving thanks to the Father who has qualified us to be partakers of the inheritance of the saints in the light" (Col. 1:11-12, NKJV).

The preceding verse is found in an intercessory prayer the Apostle Paul wrote for the Colossian Christians. He went on to pray, "He [the Father] has delivered us from the power of darkness and conveyed us into the kingdom of the Son of His love, in whom we have redemption through His blood, the forgiveness of sins" (Col. 1:13-14, NKJV).

These verses provide you with only a partial glimpse into the magnificent inheritance your Father has bequeathed you. Other parts of the Bible reveal the rest. Both the Old Testament and the New Testament point to the ". . .unsearchable riches of Christ" (Eph. 3:8, NKJV), which are your rightful inheritance as a precious child of your heavenly Father.

God's great faithfulness to you is displayed on nearly every page of the holy Scriptures, and God never forgets His promises to you. In fact, "He remembers his covenant forever, the word he commanded, for a thousand generations, . . .an everlasting covenant" (Ps. 105:8-10, NIV).

God is ever faithful to His Word. He is careful to honor all His promises and commitments to you. The Bible is a blessed book that presents the Father's covenant, bond, pledge, promise, commitment, and contract with His children in a very readable and loving way. It is His covenant with you, His dearly beloved child.

Throughout history, believers have found God's Word to be their very source, strength, destiny, and purpose, and it can be the same for you in this present day. God is active in your life. Therefore, it is totally accurate for you to understand Him in light of present-tense, active verbs. God *speaks* to you. God *loves* you. God *knows* you. God *wants* to meet all your needs. God *is* present with you. God *honors* His Word to you. God *promises* not to withhold any good thing from you. God *performs* His Word in your life. God *understands* all that you need. God *protects* you. God *sustains* you. God *upholds* you. God *is* faithful to you. God *is* your Father. Every one of these truths is amply supported throughout the Bible.

God acts according to His Word. All these wonderful blessings come to you through His Word by His Spirit, and the recipient of all these blessings is none other than you, yourself.

Take a moment right now to reflect on what it means to know God as your faithful Father, your papa God, your Abba. Let Him reveal himself to you through Jesus and His Word. Receive His full inheritance into your life and let it motivate you always to ". . .walk worthy of the Lord, fully pleasing Him, being fruitful in every good work and increasing in the knowledge of God" (Col. 1:10, NKJV).

Each new day you will see His hand at work in your life, and you will exclaim with Jeremiah, "Because His compassions fail not. They are new every morning; Great is Your faithfulness. 'The Lord is my portion,' says my soul, 'therefore I hope in Him!'" (Lam. 3:22-24, NKJV).

God Loves You!

Your personal knowledge of the constant love of God is one of the greatest spiritual resources you have available to you. He loves you far more than any earthly parent ever could. He loves you in the good times and the bad times, as well. He loves you when you obey Him, and He loves you when you wander away. God's love for you is an absolute that you can always count on. His love does not fail you when you make a mistake. It is the Father's undying love for you, His precious child, that compels Him to help you.

To understand the Father's heart, it will help to use an analogy. Let's compare the heart of God our Father with the heart of an earthly father. Most earthly fathers, though imperfect, want only the best for their children. They strive to protect their children, to meet their needs, and to keep them safe from all fear, evil, and harm. Most earthly fathers want to be a present help to their children by serving them as a role model, teacher, example, leader, counselor, and caregiver.

Your heavenly Father wants all these things for you and so many other things as well. In truth, "Eye has not seen, nor ear heard, nor have entered into the heart of man the things which God has prepared for those who love Him" (1 Cor. 2:9, NKJV). Your Father God promises to supply everything you need, and to keep on giving more and more. Paul wrote, "And my God shall supply all your need according to His riches in glory by Christ Jesus. Now to our God and Father be glory forever and ever" (Phil. 4:19-20, NKJV).

Jesus, himself, compared the Father's love to that of an earthly father. In His brilliantly beautiful Sermon on the Mount, Jesus proclaimed, "Ask, and it will be given to you; seek, and you will find; knock, and it will be opened to you. For everyone who asks receives, and he who seeks finds, and to him who knocks it will be opened. Or what man is there among you who, if his son asks for bread, will give him a stone? Or if he asks for a fish, will he give him a serpent? If you then, being evil, know how to give good gifts to your children, how much more will your Father who is in heaven give good things to those who ask Him!" (Matt. 7:7-11, NKJV).

The love of your heavenly Father touches your life in so many important ways. It redeems you, saves you, heals you, supports you, keeps you, helps you, guides you, corrects you, and blesses you. In fact, His love surrounds you at all times. This is a special part of your inheritance as a child of God.

The Bible says, "In this the love of God was manifested toward us, that God has sent His only begotten Son into the world, that we might live through Him" (1 John 4:9, NKJV).

Most earthly fathers want to protect their children. This is absolutely true of your heavenly Father. Notice the effect His love has in your life: "And we have known and believed the love that God has for us. God is love, and he who abides in love abides in God, and God in him" (1 John 4:16, NKJV).

As one of God's beloved children, always remember these words: "There is no fear in love; but perfect love [God's love] casts out fear" (1 John 4:18, NKJV). God promises that, as you experience His love, your fears will leave. It is important to your heavenly Father that you be free from fear, because fear robs you of intimacy with Him and steals your hope.

The Psalmist put it this way: "God is our refuge and strength, a very present help in time of trouble. Therefore we will not fear, even though the earth be removed, and though the mountains be carried into the midst of the sea. . . .Be still, and know that I am God" (Ps. 46.1-10, NKJV). Knowing God intimately lifts us above all fear and insecurity. As we learn to be still before Him, our relationship with Him deepens.

An intimate relationship with God gives you both a sense of security and an unwavering confidence to face anything and everything that comes your way. Without question, the inspired writers of the Scriptures were certain God would be faithful to every word He spoke. This is the only stance for a believer to take in our world today, as well. Isaiah, the ancient prophet, wrote: "The grass withers and the flowers fall, but the word of our God stands forever" (Isa. 40:8, NIV).

Complete and utter confidence in God's Word and His amazing love for you makes all the difference in the world. His is a healing, restoring, calming, encouraging love, and it is always available to you. Paul wrote, "For now we see in a mirror, dimly, but then face to face. Now I know in part, but then I shall know just as I also am known. And now abide faith, hope, love, these three; but the greatest of these is love" (1 Cor. 13:12-13, NKJV).

As we have seen, God is completely faithful to you. He loves you with an everlasting love. As your Father, He takes good care of you. He protects you and defends you. He watches out for you, and He meets your every need. He wants to spend time with you, and He is a very present help to you. He wants to teach you everything that He knows will benefit you. He guides you. He holds your hand. He lifts you up. He actually takes delight in you.

Zephaniah 3:17 says, "The Lord your God in your midst, the Mighty One, will save; He will rejoice over you with gladness, He will quiet you with His love, He will rejoice over you with singing."

This wonderful Scripture reveals how much you mean to God. No matter what you may have done, God loves you. He does not see you as your behavior—good or bad—but as His workmanship created in Christ Jesus. (See Eph. 2:10.) God, your Father, sees you fulfilling the purpose for which He created you—to love Him and be blessed by His love for you.

Jesus Reveals the Father to You

Philip said to Jesus, "Lord, show us the Father, and it is sufficient for us" (John 14:8, NKJV).

Jesus responded, "Have I been with you so long, and yet you have not known Me, Philip? He who has seen Me has seen the Father; so how can you say, 'Show us the Father'? Do you not believe that I am in the Father, and the Father in Me? The words that I speak to you I do not speak on My own authority; but the Father who dwells in Me does the works. Believe Me that I am in the Father and the Father in Me, or else believe Me for the sake of the works themselves" (John 14:9-10, NKJV).

In the life and ministry of our Lord and Savior Jesus Christ, the wisdom, power, and glory of the Father is revealed. He is the almighty Father who performs miracles. He is a loving Shepherd who deeply cares about His sheep. He is constantly at work in your life, sensitive to your every need, and deeply devoted to you. He desires a close, personal relationship with you.

Jesus said, "I am the way, the truth, and the life. No one comes to the Father except through Me. If you had known Me, you would have known My Father also; and from

now on you know Him and have seen Him"
(John 14:6-7, NKJV).

Fellowship With God

Through faith in Christ, you have access
to your heavenly Father. It is the blood of
Christ that enables you to have fellowship
with God. Paul wrote, "But God demonstrates
His own love toward us, in that while we
were still sinners, Christ died for us. Much
more then, having now been justified by His
blood, we shall be saved from wrath through
Him. For if when we were enemies we were
reconciled to God through the death of His
Son, much more, having been reconciled, we
shall be saved by His life" (Rom. 5:8-10, NKJV).

John puts it this way: "That which was
from the beginning, which we have heard,
which we have seen with our eyes, which we
have looked upon, and our hands have
handled, concerning the Word of life—the life
was manifested, and we have seen, and bear
witness, and declare to you that eternal life
which was with the Father and was manifested
to us—that which we have seen and heard we
declare to you, that you also may have fellowship
with us; and truly our fellowship is with the
Father and with His Son Jesus Christ" (1 John
1:1-3, NKJV).

You have fellowship with God the Father and with His Son, Jesus Christ. This blessed fellowship enables you to know your Father in vitally important ways. If you want to know what the Father is like, take a look at Jesus, and then draw close to the Father through Him.

"Draw near to God and He will draw near to you. . . .Humble yourselves in the sight of the Lord, and He will lift you up" (James 4:8-10, NKJV).

Yes, God is your loving Father, and He is always there to give you everything you need. Always remember these words of Jesus: "But seek the kingdom of God, and all these things shall be added to you. Do not fear, little flock, for it is your Father's good pleasure to give you the kingdom" (Luke 12:31-32, NKJV).

God Is Your Abba Father

The word *abba* appears three times in the New Testament – in Mark 14:36, Romans 8:15, and Galatians 4:6. It is an Aramaic/Syro-Chaldaic term, which is borrowed from the language of childhood in order to show strong affection, intimacy, and respect for one's father. It literally means "papa."

In the Garden of Gethsemane, on the night before His betrayal, Jesus cried, "Abba, Father, all things are possible for You. Take this cup away from Me; nevertheless, not what I will, but what You will" (Mark 14:36, NKJV). Here we see Jesus using both the Aramaic (Abba) and Greek (Father) terms to convey His submission to Father God. This speaks of the Father's love for Gentiles and Jews alike, for "Abba" is close to the Hebrew word *Ab*, which connotes filial tenderness, respect, and affection. We frequently find the word "Ab" used in compound proper names, such as Abraham, Abimelech, Abner, and Eliab.

Jesus' cry, "Abba, Father," is the believer's cry as well, for God truly is our Father, and He desires an intimate relationship with each one of us. He wants us to cry out to Him, and to believe that, as our Abba Father, He will always take care of us.

Our heavenly Father always wants the best for us, and He promises to meet each of our needs. Paul wrote, "And my God shall supply all your need according to His riches in glory by Christ Jesus" (Phil. 4:19, NKJV).

The preceding promise from the Bible comes directly from Father God's heart just as does each of the letters within this book. He wants us to take Him at His Word, to believe His promises, to receive His blessings, and to act upon His teachings.

"Abba Father" is the cry of our hearts—a cry placed within us by the Holy Spirit. The charming simplicity of these words conveys the tenderness and warmth of the Father toward us, His children. This expression also represents the desire a child has to please its father, and displays immense feelings of love, respect, honor, and devotion.

Paul wrote, "For you did not receive the spirit of bondage again to fear, but you received the Spirit of adoption by whom we cry out, 'Abba, Father'" (Rom. 8:15, NKJV). The Holy Spirit is constantly at work in our lives to draw us close to God and to reveal His will to us. This verse clearly shows us that God, our Father, wants a close personal relationship with us, His children.

In ancient times a slave was not permitted to use the term "abba" when addressing his master, because the master-slave relationship was far different from the father-son relationship. In this verse Paul is showing us that in the new birth we have received the Holy Spirit, who imparts a sense of belonging and sonship, and now we find ourselves crying, "Abba Father." We are not slaves any longer; we've been redeemed by Christ from the bondage to sin, Satan, and the Law, and we are totally free!

Our Father God has emancipated us by sending His only begotten Son, Jesus, to die for us. Because Jesus died for our sins, we are no longer slaves, but free men and women in Christ. In fact, Paul goes on, "The Spirit Himself bears witness with our spirit that we are children of God, and if children, then heirs—heirs of God and joint heirs with Christ, if indeed we suffer with Him, that we may also be glorified together" (Rom. 8:16-17, NKJV).

Through faith in Christ, we are born again and become the children of God. As His children, we are His heirs. In reality, we are joint heirs with Christ, members of God's royal family. As such, we are entitled to receive and enjoy all the rights and blessings of the Kingdom of God.

It is because we are now God's children that the Holy Spirit within us joins with our spirit, encouraging us to cry, "Abba, Father." It is a cry of gratitude and of joy, because it comes from our recognition of who God is to us (our Abba) and who we are to Him (His precious children).

In the language of sonship demonstrated by the word "abba" we have the assurance of God's tender love and affection toward us. The word helps us to know how deeply He loves us, and it enables us to express our love back to Him.

He created us, so He could love us and we could love Him back, and He ever pursues us with this desire for intimate relationship in His heart.

In his letter to the Galatians Paul wrote, "And because you are sons, God has sent forth the Spirit of His Son into your hearts, crying out, 'Abba, Father!'" (Gal. 4:6, NKJV). It is because we are God's children that the Holy Spirit cries through us, "Abba, Father." He wants us to enter into the blessings of sonship by drawing close to the God, our loving Father.

Again, Paul emphasizes the fact that we are free people in Christ, emancipated children of God: "Therefore you are no longer a slave but a son, and if a son, then an heir of God through Christ" (Gal. 4:7, NKJV).

As you read *Letters From the Heart of God*, let the Holy Spirit cry out through you, "Abba, Father." Join Him in that cry as you draw near to God. The Bible says, "Therefore submit to God. Resist the devil and he will flee from you. Draw near to God and He will draw near to you" (James 4:8, NKJV).

You will discover that this book will help you draw near to God. It is a very useful tool in your personal devotional life, a great aid to Bible study, a tremendous faith-builder, and an avenue to a close, personal relationship with Abba.

Read the letters as if He wrote them to you, personally, for they are filled with promises from His Word, which are for you to believe and receive. *Letters From the Heart of God* flow directly from the Father's heart to yours. You will notice some of the letters are signed "Abba Father," who is your heavenly "Papa" and loves you with an everlasting love. (See Jer. 31:3.)

After you read each letter, you may wish to write a personal letter of response to God in which you can express to Him your thoughts, feelings, hopes, aspirations, and requests. You may also want to make notes for future study of any special insights the letter brought to you.

May the multitude of His blessings (your inheritance as a child of God) fall upon you as you read, study, and meditate upon each of the alphabetically arranged, topical letters of this book. In these pages you will hear God speaking to you, and as this happens, be sure to remember these words, "Faith comes by hearing, and hearing by the word of God" (Rom. 10:17, NKJV).

Letters From
the
Heart of God

1

Abiding in Christ

Key Thought: Abide in Christ, and let Him abide in you. This is the key to fruitfulness in your life and ministry.

Key Scripture: *"I am the vine, you are the branches. He who abides in Me, and I in him, bears much fruit; for without Me you can do nothing"* (John 15:5, NKJV).

Letter From the Heart of God

Dear child, listen to the words of My Son, Jesus, who said, "Abide in Me, and I in you. As the branch cannot bear fruit of itself, unless it abides in the vine, neither can you, unless you abide in Me."[1] Remember that this is the key to great fruitfulness in your life and ministry.[2] As the Vinedresser, I will always be watching out for you. Remember that My pruning in your life is to help you become more fruitful.[3]

As you learn to abide in Christ and let His words abide in you, you will experience the power of answered prayer. Indeed, you will be able to ask whatever you will and it shall be done for you.[4]

Abiding in Christ is so very important, My child, because it will keep you from sin.[5] Such abiding involves settling down, taking root in Christ, and dwelling and living in Him, so please, My child, be sure always to abide in Christ.

You are My precious loved one. I ask you to seek Me at all times, because I am never far from you. The more you learn to abide in Christ, the more fully you will discover that you live and move and have your being in Me.[6] This is what I want you to know and experience every day of your life, because I love you with an everlasting love.[7]

Never forget that I am your refuge and fortress. I simply ask that you trust in Me as you abide under My shadow and dwell in the secret place of My presence.[8] As you believe on the name of My Son, Jesus Christ, and love others as He has commanded you to do, you will abide in Christ, and He will abide in you. As you do this, the Holy Spirit will bring this assurance to your heart.[9]

Therefore, I beseech you to abide in Christ each moment of every day.

Many blessings and much love,

Your Abba Father

References: *(1) John 15:4; (2) John 15:5; (3) John 15:1-2; (4) John 15:7; (5) 1 John 3:6; (6) Acts 17:28; (7) Jeremiah 31:3; (8) Psalms 91:1; (9) 1 John 3:23-24.*

2
Abundant Life

Key Thought: Abundance in every area of your life is God's desire for you.

Key Scripture: *"The thief does not come except to steal, and to kill, and to destroy. I have come that they may have life, and that they may have it more abundantly"* (John 10:10, NKJV).

Letter From the Heart of God

Dearly beloved, I want you to prosper in all things and be in health, just as your soul prospers.[1] I want you to experience the abundant life Jesus promises to you.[2] I want your cup to overflow,[3] and your joy to be full.[4] It is My great pleasure to give you My kingdom.[5]

As your Father, I want you to know that I care about every part of your life. Therefore, I invite you to cast all your cares on Me.[6] I always want the best for you, and I am able and always willing to supply all of your needs according to My riches in glory through Christ Jesus.[7]

I want you to be able to find your delight in the abundance of My peace.[8] Therefore, I ask you to seek first My kingdom and My righteousness, and, as you do so, you will

soon discover that everything in your life will
be taken care of.[9]

My joy is your strength.[10] My grace will
always be sufficient for you.[11] Remember that
My divine power has already given you all
things that pertain to both life and godliness
through My Son, Jesus.[12] My child, receive the
inheritance I've provided for you,[13] and enjoy
the abundance I give every day of your life.
Receive it by faith.[14]

With abundant blessings,

God, your Father

References: *(1) 3 John 2; (2) John 10:10; (3) Psalms 23:5;*
(4) John 15:11; (5) Luke 12:32; (6) 1 Peter 5:7; (7)
Philippians 4:19; (8) Psalms 37:11; (9) Matthew 6:33; (10)
Nehemiah 8:10; (11) 2 Corinthians 12:9; (12) 2 Peter 1:3;
(13) Ephesians 1:17-18; (14) Romans 1:17.

Now you may wish to write a letter of personal
response to God.

3

Achievement

Key Thought: Through faith you are enabled to achieve great things.

Key Scripture: *"I delight to do Your will, O my God, and Your law is within my heart"* (Ps. 40:8, NKJV).

Letter From the Heart of God

My precious child, as you endeavor to do well[1] and to please Me,[2] I promise to enable and empower you to do great things in My name.[3] Indeed, you shall become a mighty person of valor,[4] and I will make you more than a conqueror through Christ.[5] It is My desire to make you an able minister of the New Testament.[6]

Never forget that I am able to make all grace abound toward you,[7] and My grace shall always be sufficient for you.[8] As you learn to trust in Me,[9] you will discover that I am able to do exceedingly abundantly above all you can ask or think.[10] Therefore, it will be My strength that will enable you to become an achiever in all your endeavors.

What I promise to you, My child, I am able to accomplish.[11] Through Christ you can do all things, because He will strengthen you.[12] My strength will be made perfect in your time of weakness.[13] Always remember that I am the God of all grace, and I have called you to My eternal glory by Christ Jesus.

I will perfect, establish, strengthen, and settle you,[14] for I am working in you both to will and to accomplish my good pleasure and purpose in your life.[15] You can accomplish all I've called you to do, because I have begun a good work in you and I will carry it on to completion until the day of Jesus Christ,[16] for you are complete in Him.[17] Believe My Word.

With love,

Your faithful Father

References: *(1) Genesis 4:7; (2) 1 Corinthians 7:32; (3) John 5:20; (4) Joshua 6:2; (5) Romans 8:37; (6) 2 Corinthians 3:6; (7) 2 Corinthians 9:8; (8) 2 Corinthians 12:9; (9) Proverbs 3:5-6; (10) Ephesians 3:20; (11) Romans 4:21; (12) Philippians 4:13; (13) 2 Corinthians 12:9; (14) 1 Peter 5:10; (15) Philippians 2:13; (16) Philippians 1:6; (17) Colossians 2:10.*

Now you may wish to write a letter of personal response to God.

4

Addictions

Key Thought: Every addiction comes between you and God.

Key Scripture: *"Stand fast therefore in the liberty wherewith Christ hath made us free, and be not entangled again with the yoke of bondage"* (Gal. 5:1).

Letter From the Heart of God

My dearly loved child, I have sent Jesus to sever every chain that holds you back from your rightful freedom as My very own child.[1] His anointing in your life has the power to break every yoke in your life.[2] Enter into the glorious liberty I have provided for My children.[3] Stand fast in the liberty Christ has given to you, and don't ever allow yourself to be entangled with a yoke of bondage again.[4]

Remember, My child, whatever you think of yourself in your heart is what you will be.[5] Do not identify yourself according to your behavior, for I don't. Never forget that you are My workmanship, created in Christ Jesus for good works.[6] This is how I think of you, My child. As you see yourself loved and accepted by Me, healing will come to your heart, and you will no longer need your addiction to make life bearable.

It is My desire to make you a blessing, and to cause showers of blessing to fall upon you.[7] Come to Me, so that I will be able to heal your bruises and bind up your broken heart.[8] Let My tender, loving care become a part of your life.[9] Truly, I am able to meet all the needs of your life, and I want to meet each need you have.[10] My child, let Me do so now.

It will delight My heart to be able to restore hope to you,[11] and to impart joy,[12] a renewed sense of purpose,[13] and abundant life to you,[14] My child.

Remember, I am your Father, and you are My child. You are the apple of My eye.[15] Therefore, turn from your addiction and return to Me.[16] In returning and resting in Me, you will be healed; in quietness and trusting confidence shall be your strength.[17]

I love you,

Your heavenly Father

References: (1) Luke 4:18; (2) Ezekiel 34:27; (3) Romans 8:21; (4) Galatians 5:1; (5) Proverbs 23:7; (6) Ephesians 2:10; (7) Ezekiel 34:26; (8) Isaiah 61:1; (9) 1 Peter 5:7; (10) Philippians 4:19; (11) Romans 8:24; (12) Nehemiah 8:10; (13) Romans 8:28; (14) John 10:10; (15) Psalms 17:8; (16) Isaiah 35:10; (17) Isaiah 30:15.

5
Anger

Key Thought: The word "anger" is only one letter short of the word "danger."

Key Scripture: *"So then, my beloved brethren, let every man be swift to hear, slow to speak, slow to wrath; for the wrath of man does not produce the righteousness of God"* (James 1:19-20, NKJV).

Letter From the Heart of God

Dearly beloved, the anger you feel comes from the hurts and frustrations you are experiencing. Allow Me to be the Healer of all your inner hurts, frustrations, and disappointments.[1] Cease from your anger and forsake your wrath.[2] Come to Me.[3] Never forget that I love you, My child.[4]

Let My grace enable you to forgive those who have hurt you.[5] Lay aside all hurt feelings, and receive with meekness My Word, which contains the power to restore you to wholeness and to save your soul.[6] Obey My Word, and put away your anger, wrath, and bad feelings toward others.[7]

In Christ, you are a new creation. The old things have passed away, and all things have become new.[8] Therefore, be clothed with your new self, which is renewed in knowledge according to My image.[9]

My child, I ask you to renounce any power anger has held over you and to repent of any sins into which it has led you. Never let the sun go down upon your anger.[10] When possible, always make it right with the persons with whom you have conflicts.[11]

When you are angry turn to Me, and I will restore your soul and guide you in the path of righteousness for My name's sake.[12] My Word will be a lamp unto your feet and a light unto your path.[13] Give no place to the devil.[14]

Be careful what you say. Let no corrupt or evil words proceed from your mouth, but speak what is good and edifying, so your words will minister grace both to you and others.[15] Remember that a wholesome tongue is a tree of life,[16] and the power of life and death is in the tongue.[17]

Never forget that a soft answer will turn wrath away.[18] When you learn to be slow to anger, My child, you will be better than the mighty, and when you learn to rule your own spirit, you will be better than he who takes a city.[19]

Therefore, get rid of all bitterness, wrath, and anger. Replace those responses with the fruit of the Holy Spirit, which is love, peace, joy, patience, meekness, gentleness, goodness, and self-control.[20] Be kind to others, tender-hearted and forgiving, in the same way that I have forgiven you for Christ's sake.[21]

Peace be yours,

Your heavenly Father

References: (1) Exodus 15:26; (2) Psalms 37:8; (3) Matthew 11:28; (4) 1 John 4:10; (5) Colossians 3:13; (6) James 1:21; (7) Colossians 3:8; (8) 2 Corinthians 5:17; (9) Colossians 3:10; (10) Ephesians 4:26; (11) Matthew 5:23-24; (12) Psalms 23:3; (13) Psalms 119:105; (14) Ephesians 4:27; (15) Ephesians 4:29; (16) Proverbs 15:4; (17) Proverbs 18:21; (18) Proverbs 15:1; (19) Proverbs 16:32; (20) Galatians 5:22-23; (21) Ephesians 4:32.

Now you may wish to write a letter of personal response to God.

6

Anxiety

Key Thought: God wants you to give your anxieties, worries, and fear to Him.

Key Scripture: *"Casting all your care upon Him, for He cares for you"* (1 Pet. 5:7, NKJV).

Letter From the Heart of God

My child, I want you to know that you have no reason to be anxious or fearful about anything, because My perfect love casts all fear away from you.[1] Don't let your heart be troubled; believe in Me with all your heart.[2] Jesus has imparted His peace to you; therefore, don't be afraid about anything.[3]

Be anxious for nothing, my child, but in everything by prayer and supplication, with thanksgiving, let your requests be made known to Me. Then you will experience My peace, a peace that surpasses all understanding, and My peace will keep your heart and mind through Christ Jesus.[4]

Therefore, instead of worrying and being anxious, meditate on whatever things are noble, just, pure, lovely and of good report.[5] Keep your mind stayed on Me at all times, and trust in Me, because this will give you perfect peace.[6] Always remember that I am your Shepherd, and because this is true, you will never experience want.[7]

I make you to lie down in green pastures, and I lead you beside still waters. I restore your soul, and I lead you in the paths of righteousness for My name's sake. Yes, it's true, My child, and even if you should walk through the valley of the shadow of death you will fear no evil, because you will know that I am always with you. My rod and my staff will give you comfort. Surely goodness and mercy shall follow you all the days of your life, and you will dwell in My house forever.[8] I am taking care of you, My child.

Peace and joy to you,

Your loving Father

References: (1) 1 John 4:18; (2) John 14:1; (3) John 14:27; (4) Philippians 4:6-7; (5) Philippians 4:8; (6) Isaiah 26:3; (7) Psalms 23:1; (8) Psalms 23:2-6.

Now you may wish to write a letter of personal response to God.

7

Attitudes

Key Thought: The Beatitudes reveal what our attitudes should be toward God, others, and ourselves.

Key Scripture: *"Let this mind be in you which was also in Christ Jesus"* (Phil. 2:5, NKJV).

Letter From the Heart of God

My dear child, keep a watch over your heart with all diligence, because it is from your heart that the issues of life proceed.[1] Give attention to My Word, and incline your ear to My sayings.[2] Do not let them depart from your eyes, and keep them in the midst of your heart,[3] for My Word is life and health to you.[4]

Let the mind of Christ be in you to guide you and direct your steps.[5] Remember the words of Jesus, who said that the poor in spirit, those who mourn, the meek, those who hunger and thirst for righteousness, the merciful, the pure in heart, the peacemakers, and those who are persecuted for righteousness' sake are blessed.

Let these attitudes be yours, My child, because they will give so much. You will partake of the Kingdom of heaven, My comfort, My righteousness, and My mercy.

Indeed, you will inherit the earth, you will see Me, and you will be called My child.[6]

Therefore, I beseech you, dear one, let all bitterness, wrath, anger, clamor, and evil speaking be put away from you, with all malice. And be kind to others, tenderhearted, forgiving others, even as I have forgiven you in Christ.[7]

Fulfill My joy by being like-minded with your fellow-believers, having the same love, being of one accord, of one mind, and don't ever do anything out of selfish ambition or conceit. In lowliness of mind esteem others as better than yourself. Look out for the interests of others as well as your own interests.[8]

Let My love guide you in all things, and remember that love suffers long and is kind. Love does not envy. Love does not parade itself, and is not puffed up. Love never behaves rudely, and does not seek its own. Love is not provoked, and it thinks no evil. Love never rejoices in iniquity, but always rejoices in the truth. Love bears all things, believes all things, hopes all things, and endures all things. Beloved, love never fails,[9] so let love be the attitude of your heart at all times.

With all My love,

Your heavenly Father

References: *(1) Proverbs 4:23; (2) Proverbs 4:20; (3) Proverbs 4:21; (4) Proverbs 4:22; (5) Philippians 2:5; (6) Matthew 5:3-11; (7) Ephesians 4:31-32; (8) Philippians 2:2-4; (9) 1 Corinthians 13:4-8.*

Now you may wish to write a letter of personal response to God.

8

Authority Over the Enemy

Key Thought: Divine authority is yours through Christ.

Key Scripture: *"And they overcame him by the blood of the Lamb, and by the word of their testimony; and they loved not their lives unto the death"* (Rev. 12:11).

Letter From the Heart of God

My child, I have given all authority in heaven and on earth to Jesus, My Son. As a believer, authority has been delegated to you, and you have been commissioned to go forth in Jesus' name, to share the good news with others, and to teach them My will.[1]

I have given you the authority to be victorious over the enemy in every area of your life.[2] This authority is exercised through the name of Jesus;[3] the blood of Jesus;[4] My holy Word, which is the sword of the Spirit;[5] the empowerment of the Holy Spirit;[6] steadfast faith;[7] and fervent prayer.[8]

Do not be afraid,[9] for I will guide you daily regarding how to walk in spiritual authority in every situation you face.[10] Assuredly, I say to you that whatever you bind on earth will be bound in heaven, and whatever you loose on earth will be loosed in heaven. If you agree with at least one other believer concerning anything you are praying about, I promise to do it for you. Always remember that, where two or three are gathered together in the name of Jesus Christ, He will be in your midst.[11]

My child, it is not by your own might or power that you will be able to exercise My authority in any given circumstance, but it is by My Spirit that you shall always prevail.[12] Therefore, be continually filled with the Holy Spirit[13] and let Him work through you.[14]

Remember, My child, that the weapons I have given you are not carnal, but they are mighty through Me for the pulling down of evil strongholds.[15] Be sure to put on all the armor I have given you, My child, so you will be able to stand against the wiles of the devil.[16]

Because I must resist the proud, but always give grace to the humble, I urge you to humble yourself under My mighty hand.[17] Submit to me, My child; resist the devil, and he will flee from you.[18] Be sober, be vigilant; because your adversary, the devil, walks about like a roaring lion, seeking whom he may devour. My child, resist him, steadfast in the faith.[19]

Cast all your care upon Me, for I care for you,[20] and always remember that I will never leave you nor forsake you.[21]

Many blessings and much love,

God, your Father

References: *(1) Matthew 28:18-20; (2) Luke 10:19; (3) Mark 16:17; (4) Revelation 12:11; (5) Ephesians 6:17; (6) Acts 1:8; (7) 1 Peter 5:8-9; (8) James 5:16; (9) Deuteronomy 31:8; (10) Romans 8:14; (11) Matthew 18:18-21; (12) Zechariah 4:6; (13) Ephesians 5:18; (14) Ephesians 3:20; (15) 2 Corinthians 10:4; (16) Ephesians 6:11-18; (17) 1 Peter 5:5-6; (18) James 4:7; (19) 1 Peter 5:9; (20) 1 Peter 5:7; (21) Hebrews 13:5.*

Now you may wish to write a letter of personal response to God.

9

Backsliding

Key Thought: Backsliding is losing ground to the enemy.

Key Scripture: *"Return, you backsliding children, and I will heal your backslidings. Indeed we do come to You, for You are the Lord our God"* (Jer. 3:22, NKJV).

Letter From the Heart of God

My child, I am concerned about you, because I have seen the way you are living. That's why I am writing, to ask you to return to Me, so that I can heal your backsliding.[1]

It's because I love you that I want you to come to Me, for I have the power to restore health to you, and to heal you of all your wounds.[2] Let Me heal you and reveal to you the abundance of peace and truth I have in store for you.[3]

My backslidden child, remember that I am your Father.[4] I will give you shepherds according to My heart, who will feed you with knowledge and understanding.[5]

I don't want you to be tossed to and fro and carried about with every wind of doctrine, by the trickery of men, in the cunning craftiness of deceitful plotting. My fatherly desire for you is that you would speak the truth in love, and grow up in all things into Christ, who is the head of His body, the Church.[6]

Do not walk any longer as many others walk, in the futility of their minds, having their understanding darkened and being alienated from My life. They are ignorant and blind. Being past feeling, they have given themselves over to lewdness, to work all uncleanness with greediness.[7]

Remember, My child, that you have not so learned Christ. You have heard Him and have been taught by Him. Therefore, as your loving Father, I implore you to put off the old, unrenewed self, which grows corrupt according to deceitful lusts and desires, and be renewed in the attitudes of your mind. Put on the new self, which was created after My likeness in true righteousness and holiness.[8]

My goodness is leading you to repent[9] with godly sorrow.[10] Do not run from Me, My child, run to Me. I want to restore you to intimate fellowship with Me.[11] Therefore, I urge you to repent of your sins, confessing them to Me now, and I will forgive you and cleanse you from all unrighteousness.[12]

Return to fellowship with Me, for I miss you.

Grace and peace to you,

Your loving and forgiving Father

References: *(1) Jeremiah 3:22; (2) Jeremiah 30:17; (3) Jeremiah 33:6; (4) Jeremiah 3:14; (5) Jeremiah 3:15; (6) Ephesians 4:14-16; (7) Ephesians 4:17-19; (8) Ephesians 4:20-24; (9) Romans 2:4; (10) 2 Corinthians 7:10; (11) 1 John 1:6; (12) 1 John 1:9.*

Now you may wish to write a letter of personal response to God.

10

Bitterness

Key Thought: Let the circumstances of life make you better, not bitter.

Key Scripture: *"Pursue peace with all people, and holiness, without which no one will see the Lord: looking carefully lest anyone fall short of the grace of God; lest any root of bitterness springing up cause trouble, and by this many become defiled"* (Heb. 12:14-15, NKJV).

Letter From the Heart of God

My dear child, the opposite of bitterness is sweetness, and I want you to experience My sweetness in place of your bitterness. Come! Taste and see that I am good.[1]

Pursue peace and holiness at all times and with all people so you will not fall short of My grace. If you permit a root of bitterness to spring up in your life, it will cause you and others much trouble.[2] This is not My will for you.

My child, your heart knows the extent of your bitterness.[3] Therefore, I ask you to examine your heart, and to repent of any bitterness you find there.[4] As you confess your sins to Me, I will forgive you and cleanse you from all unrighteousness, including bitterness.[5]

Take heed to My Word, for it is sweet.[6] You will find that My Word is sweeter than honey, and it will be the perfect antidote to your bitterness.[7] Sing to Me, My child, sing praise to Me.[8] Let your meditation of Me and My Word bring sweetness to your soul. This will enable you to be glad in Me.[9]

My child, remember that a spring cannot send forth both fresh and bitter water from the same opening.[10] If you allow Me to do so, I will lead you into triumph over your bitterness, through Christ. Through you, I will spread the fragrance of the knowledge of myself, for you are the fragrance of Christ among those who are being saved and among those who are perishing.[11] It is for this reason that you must put all bitterness behind you, My child, and let the fragrance of Christ surround you at all times.

I love you,

Your heavenly Father

References: (1) Psalms 34:8; (2) Hebrews 12:14-15; (3) Proverbs 14:10; (4) Matthew 3:2; (5) 1 John 1:9; (6) Psalms 141:6; (7) Psalms 119:103; (8) Psalms 104:33; (9) Psalms 104:34; (10) James 3:11; (11) 2 Corinthians 2:14-15.

11
Blessings

Key Thought: God wants to bless His children at all times.

Key Scripture: *"And Jabez called on the God of Israel saying, 'Oh, that You would bless me indeed, and enlarge my territory, that Your hand would be with me, and that You would keep me from evil, that I may not cause pain!' So God granted him what he requested"* (1 Chron. 4:10, NKJV).

Letter From the Heart of God

Dear child, as Jabez learned, I want to bless you indeed.[1] Because you put Me first in your life, I will command My blessing upon you.[2] I will bless your storehouse and all that you set your hand to. I will bless you, as you learn to obey and trust Me in all things.[3] Indeed, I will cause showers of blessing to fall upon you.[4]

All My blessings, My child, shall come upon you and overtake you, as you obey My voice and believe My Word.[5] You shall be blessed in the country and in the city.[6] I will bless you as you come in and when you go out.[7] I will cause your enemies who rise against you to be defeated before your face.[8]

My dear child, I am opening to you My good treasure.[9] It is My will and desire to make you the head and not the tail. You shall be above only, and not be beneath, if you heed My commandments.[10] As My child, you are entitled to the inheritance I have provided for you.

Remember that I have already blessed you with every spiritual blessing in the heavenly places in Christ.[11] It is always My good pleasure to give you the blessings of My kingdom.[12] I have transferred you out of the power of darkness into the Kingdom of the Son of My love,[13] and all of My promises are yes and amen in Jesus Christ your Lord.[14]

Many blessings and much love,

Your Abba Father

References: *(1) 1 Chronicles 4:10; (2) Leviticus 25:21; (3) Deuteronomy 28:8-9; (4) Ezekiel 34:26; (5) Deuteronomy 28:2; (6) Deuteronomy 28:3; (7) Deuteronomy 28:6; (8) Deuteronomy 28:7; (9) Deuteronomy 28:12; (10) Deuteronomy 28:13; (11) Ephesians 1:3; (12) Luke 12:32; (13) Colossians 1:13; (14) 2 Corinthians 1:20.*

Now you may wish to write a letter of personal response to God.

12

Blood of Christ

Key Thought: There is wonder-working power in the blood of Jesus.

Key Scripture: *"But God demonstrates His own love toward us, in that while we were still sinners, Christ died for us. Much more then, having now been justified by His blood, we shall be saved from wrath through Him"* (Rom. 5:8 9, NKJV).

Letter From the Heart of God

My dearly loved child, I sent Jesus, My only begotten Son, to earth to be a sacrifice for your sins. Your faith in Him gives you ever-lasting life.[1] It is because I love you that I sent Jesus to die for you.[2] His blood justifies you,[3] gives you peace,[4] and redeems you from the hands of the enemy.[5]

Always remember that you were not redeemed with corruptible things, such as silver, gold, or money, but with the precious blood of Christ, as of a lamb without blemish and without spot.[6]

When you walk in the light, as Jesus and I are in the light, you will have fellowship with other believers and with Us, and the blood of Jesus Christ, My Son, cleanses you from all sin.[7]

Jesus is the faithful witness, the firstborn from the dead, and the ruler over the kings of the earth. He loves you, and He has washed you from your sins in His own blood. As a result of this miracle, He has made you and all believers members of His kingdom and priests unto Me.[8]

The great dragon, that serpent of old, called the devil and Satan, is deceiving the whole world. He is the accuser of the brethren. But, never forget, you will overcome him by the blood of the Lamb, My Son, Jesus Christ, and by the word of your testimony.[9] My child, avail yourself of the power you find in and through the blood of Jesus.

Grace and peace to you,

Your loving Father

References: *(1) John 3:16; (2) Romans 5:8-9; (3) Romans 5:9; (4) Colossians 1:20; (5) Revelation 12:11; (6) 1 Peter 1:18-19; (7) 1 John 1:7; (8) Revelation 1:5-6; (9) Revelation 12:9-11.*

Now you may wish to write a letter of personal response to God.

13
Boldness

Key Thought: In and through Christ, you have holy boldness.

Key Scripture: *"The wicked flee when no one pursues, but the righteous are bold as a lion"* (Prov. 28:1, NKJV).

Letter From the Heart of God

My precious child, through the righteousness I've imparted to you in Christ, you will be as bold as a lion.[1] Receive this boldness now, and you will find that you are able to speak forth My Word without fear.[2] In Christ you have boldness and access with confidence through faith in Him.[3]

Have confidence in Me, My child, not in the flesh.[4] Hold fast to the confidence and hope I give to you to the end. This will enable you to rejoice at all times.[5] And remember always to come boldly to My throne of grace so that you will obtain mercy and find grace to help in your time of need.[6] Through Christ you have access by the Spirit to Me.[7] This fact should give you boldness and confidence at all times.

With all boldness, My child, let Christ be magnified in your body.[8] Do not be afraid of sudden terror, nor of trouble from the wicked when it comes, for I will be your confidence, and I will keep your foot from being caught.[9] Always remember that it is better to trust in Me than to put confidence in others.[10] Therefore, do not cast away your confidence, which has great reward. You have need of endurance, so that after you have done My will, you may receive what I have promised.[11]

With great love,

Your heavenly Father

References: *(1) Proverbs 28:1; (2) Philippians 1:14; (3) Ephesians 3:12; (4) Philippians 3:3-4; (5) Hebrews 3:6; (6) Hebrews 4:16; (7) Ephesians 2:18; (8) Philippians 1:20; (9) Proverbs 3:25-26; (10) Psalms 118:8-9; (11) Hebrews 10:35-36.*

Now you may wish to write a letter of personal response to God.

14
Calling

Key Thought: God has called you out of the world so that you can go into the world as His ambassador.

Key Scripture: *"I, therefore, the prisoner of the Lord, beseech you to walk worthy of the calling with which you were called, with all lowliness and gentleness, with longsuffering, bearing with one another in love"* (Eph. 4:1, NKJV).

Letter From the Heart of God

My beloved one, Jesus has chosen you as His own, so you would go forth and bear much fruit. Your fruit shall remain, and whatever you ask Me in the name of Jesus I will give to you.[1] As you labor for Me, remember that all things will work together for your good, because I have called you and I know you love Me.[2] My gifts and calling in your life are irrevocable.[3]

I have called you to peace.[4] My child, always endeavor to walk worthy of the calling with which you have been called, with all lowliness and gentleness, with longsuffering, bearing with others in love.[5]

It is My desire, beloved, to give you the spirit of wisdom and revelation in the deep and intimate knowledge of Me. This will enable the eyes of your understanding to be enlightened, and you will know and understand the hope of My calling and how rich is the glory of My inheritance in the saints.[6]

There is one body and one Spirit, just as you were called in one hope of your calling.[7] Keep on pressing toward the goal for the prize of My upward call in Christ Jesus.[8]

As I count you worthy of My calling, dear child, I promise to fulfill in your life all the good pleasure of My goodness. By My power I will complete every work of your faith, that the name of Jesus Christ may be glorified in you, and you in Him, according to My grace.[9]

Bless you, My child,

Your loving Father

References: (1) John 15:16; (2) Romans 8:28; (3) Romans 11:29; (4) 1 Corinthians 7:15; (5) Ephesians 4:1; (6) Ephesians 1:17-18; (7) Ephesians 4:4; (8) Philippians 3:14; (9) 2 Thessalonians 1:11-12.

Now you may wish to write a letter of personal response to God.

15

Cheerfulness

Key Thought: The most cheerful thought of all – God loves you!

Key Scripture: *"These things I have spoken to you, that in Me you may have peace. In the world you will have tribulation; but be of good cheer, I have overcome the world"* (John 16:33, NKJV).

Letter From the Heart of God

My dear child, as you remember the truth that Jesus has truly overcome the world, your heart will be filled with joy and cheer.[1] The joy I impart to you will always translate as strength in your life.[2]

The genuineness of your faith pleases Me, My child, because it is much more precious than gold that perishes. May it ever be found to praise, honor, and glory at the revelation of Jesus Christ, whom having not seen you love. Though now you do not see Him, yet believing, you rejoice with joy inexpressible and full of glory.[3]

Let your heart be merry, My child, because a merry heart results in a cheerful countenance.[4] Show mercy to others, with cheerfulness.[5] Whenever you give, always do it cheerfully, for I love a cheerful giver.[6]

When you pray, be sure to do so in the name of Jesus, that you may receive your answer, and your joy may be full.[7] Rejoice always, pray without ceasing, in everything give thanks; for this is My will in Christ Jesus for you.[8]

As you rejoice, be sure to put your trust in Me. This will lead you ever to shout for joy, because you will realize that I'm always defending you. Love My name, dear one, and be joyful in Me. I promise to bless you and to surround you with favor as with a shield.[9]

Come to My altar, dear child, for there you will discover that I am your exceeding joy, and you shall praise Me.[10] Never forget that I am the help of your countenance and your God.[11]

Cheerfully,

Your heavenly Father

References: *(1) John 16:33; (2) Nehemiah 8:10; (3) 1 Peter 1:7-8; (4) Proverbs 15:13; (5) Romans 12:8; (6) 2 Corinthians 9:7; (7) John 16:24; (8) 1 Thessalonians 5:16-18; (9) Psalms 5:11-12; (10) Psalms 43:4; (11) Psalms 43:5.*

Now you may wish to write a letter of personal response to God.

16

Comfort

Key Thought: God is the Father of all comfort.

Key Scripture: *"For the Lord will comfort Zion, He will comfort all her waste places; He will make her wilderness like Eden, and her desert like the garden of the Lord; joy and gladness will be found in it, thanksgiving and the voice of melody"* (Isa. 51:3, NKJV).

Letter From the Heart of God

My child, turn to Me for the comfort you need, for I am the Father of mercies and the God of all comfort.[1] It is My joy to comfort you in all the tribulations you go through, so you will be able to comfort others with the same comfort I've given to you.[2] I desire to make your wilderness like Eden, and your desert like My garden, where you will find joy, gladness, thanksgiving, and the voice of melody.[3]

I have given you the Holy Spirit to be your Comforter and Helper. He is the Spirit of truth. He is in you and He will abide with you forever.[4] He will guide you and teach you all things, and He will bring to your remembrance the things I have said to you.[5]

Always remember, My child, that I love you and have given you everlasting consolation and good hope by My grace. I want to comfort your heart and establish you in every good word and work.[6]

I am your Shepherd, and, because this is true, you will never suffer want.[7] I am making you lie down in green pastures, and I am leading you beside the still waters.[8] I am restoring your soul, and I am leading you in the paths of righteousness for My name's sake.[9]

Even when you walk through the valley of the shadow of death, you will fear no evil because you will realize that I am with you. My rod and My staff will bring comfort to you.[10] I will prepare a table before you in the presence of your enemies. I will anoint your head with oil, and your cup will overflow.[11]

Surely goodness and mercy shall follow you all the days of your life, and you will dwell in My house forever and ever.[12] Let these words give you the comfort you need, My child.

Comfort and peace to you,

Your Abba Father

References: *(1) 2 Corinthians 1:3; (2) 2 Corinthians 1:4; (3) Isaiah 51:3; (4) John 14:16-17; (5) John 14:26; (6) 2 Thessalonians 2:16-17; (7) Psalms 23:1; (8) Psalms 23:2; (9) Psalms 23:3; (10) Psalms 23:4; (11) Psalms 23:5; (12) Psalms 23:6.*

17

Commitment

Key Thought: Commitment is a conscious choice.

Key Scripture: *"Nevertheless I am not ashamed, for I know whom I have believed, and am persuaded that He is able to keep what I have committed unto Him until that Day"* (2 Tim. 1:12, NKJV).

Letter From the Heart of God

My dear child, hold fast to My Word in the faith and love you find in Christ Jesus.[1] Commit your life to Me, and remain certain that I am able to keep you until the Day of Christ. Always remember that I am committed to you, and you can count on that.[2]

Commit your soul to Me in doing good, because I am your faithful Creator, your Father, your God.[3] Because you are in Christ, you are a new creation. Old things are passed away and all things have become new. Dear one, I have reconciled you to myself through Jesus Christ, and I have given you the ministry of reconciliation.[4] Commit your life and ministry to Me.

By My mercies to you, I beseech you to present your body as a holy and living sacrifice to Me, because this is your reasonable service.[5] Do not be conformed to this world, but be transformed by the renewing of your mind, so that you will be able to prove what My good, acceptable, and perfect will is.[6] This is what commitment is all about, My child.

Always be sure to guard all that I've committed to your trust. Avoid profane and idle babblings and contradictions of what is falsely called knowledge.[7] Trust in Me with all your heart, and don't lean on your own understanding. In all your ways acknowledge Me, and I promise to direct your paths.[8]

Never forget that I am able to do exceedingly abundantly above all that you can ask or think according to My power which is at work within you and through you.[9] Therefore, My child, be strong in the grace you find in Christ Jesus.[10]

In loving commitment,

Your faithful Father

References: (1) 2 Timothy 1:13; (2) 2 Timothy 1:12; (3) 1 Peter 4:19; (4) 2 Corinthians 5:17-18; (5) Romans 12:1; (6) Romans 12:2; (7) 1 Timothy 6:20; (8) Proverbs 3:5-6; (9) Ephesians 3:20; (10) 2 Timothy 2:1.

18

Compassion

Key Thought: Compassion is love in action.

Key Scripture: *"Thus says the Lord of hosts: execute true justice, show mercy and compassion everyone to his brother"* (Zech. 7:9, NKJV).

Letter From the Heart of God

Dearly beloved, I am your Rock, your Most High God, and your Redeemer.[1] I am full of compassion and forgiveness.[2] My compassions never fail. In fact, they are new every morning. I will always be faithful and compassionate toward you, My child.[3] Therefore, I want you to be like Me, showing forth mercy and compassion upon all others.[4]

I am your portion. Hope in Me.[5] I promise to be good to you as you wait for Me and seek Me.[6] This is what compassion is all about. I want you to practice compassion toward your fellow-believers. Love as brothers and sisters, be tenderhearted, be courteous.[7]

Do not return evil for evil or reviling for reviling. On the contrary, bless others, knowing that you were called to inherit My blessing.[8]

Strengthen your hands and knees, and make straight paths for your feet.[9] Pursue peace with all people, and holiness, without which no one will see Me.[10]

Love your enemies, do good, and lend, hoping for nothing in return, and your reward will be great.[11] Practice compassion and mercy at all times, just as I am compassionate and merciful.[12]

In love and compassion,

Your heavenly Father

References: *(1) Psalms 78:35; (2) Psalms 78:38; (3) Lamentations 3:22-23; (4) Zechariah 7:9; (5) Lamentations 3:24; (6) Lamentations 3:25; (7) 1 Peter 3:8; (8) 1 Peter 3:9; (9) Hebrews 12:12; (10) Hebrews 12:14; (11) Luke 6:35; (12) Luke 6:36.*

Now you may wish to write a letter of personal response to God.

19

Confession of Sins

Key Thought: Confession cleanses us of our sins.

Key Scripture: *"If we confess our sins, He is faithful and just to forgive us our sins and to cleanse us from all unrighteousness"* (1 John 1:9, NKJV).

Letter From the Heart of God

My child, always remember to confess your sins to Me. In so doing you will discover My faithfulness in forgiving your sins and cleansing you from all unrighteousness.[1] I am light, and in Me you will find no darkness at all.[2]

I want to have close fellowship with you, so please walk in the light as I am in the light.[3] As you do this, the blood of Jesus Christ will cleanse you from all sin.[4]

Know, dear child, that, as the heavens are high above the earth, so great is My mercy toward you, because you reverence Me. As far as the east is from the west, that is how far I remove your sins from you when you confess them. I have loving compassion for you, My child.[5]

You are precious to Me; therefore, I write these things to you so you will avoid sin. However, if you sin, remember that you do have an Advocate with Me, who is Jesus

Christ, the Righteous One.[6] He willingly became the sacrifice for your sins.[7]

In fact, Jesus, who knew no sin, became sin for you, so that in Him you could become endued with My righteousness and be an example of My righteousness.[8] Your Lord Jesus Christ has become your wisdom, your righteousness, your sanctification, and your redemption.[9]

My child, awake to righteousness, and do not sin.[10] Learn to do good. Seek justice. Rebuke the oppressor.[11] Come now, and let us reason together. Though your sins are like scarlet, they shall be as white as snow. Though they are red like crimson, they shall be as wool.[12]

The key, My child, is confession of your sins. Remember, if you are willing and obedient you shall eat the good of the land.[13]

With tender love,

Your forgiving Father

References: *(1) 1 John 1:9; (2) 1 John 1:5; (3) 1 John 1:6-7; (4) 1 John 1:7; (5) Psalms 103:11-13; (6) 1 John 2:1; (7) 1 John 2:2; (8) 2 Corinthians 5:21; (9) 1 Corinthians 1:30; (10) 1 Corinthians 15:34; (11) Isaiah 1:16-17; (12) Isaiah 1:18; (13) Isaiah 1:18-19.*

Now you may wish to write a letter of personal response to God.

20

Contentment

Key Thought: Contentment comes from knowing God as the One who satisfies our every need.

Key Scripture: *"Now godliness with contentment is great gain"* (1 Tim. 6:6, NKJV).

Letter From the Heart of God

My child, godliness with contentment is great gain for you.[1] As you draw close to Me and get to know Me better, I will multiply My grace and peace to you.[2] In fact, My divine power has given you all things that pertain to life and godliness.[3]

My exceedingly great and precious promises enable you to partake of My divine nature, and this will bring great contentment to your heart.[4] Learn to come into My presence and let Me show you the path of life, for there you will find fullness of joy and, at My right hand, pleasures forevermore.[5]

Like My apostle Paul, I want you to learn to be content in whatever state you find yourself.[6] In knowing both how to be abased and how to abound, you will discover that you can do all things through Christ, who strengthens you.[7] You will discover true contentment as you, through faith, realize that I shall indeed supply all your need according to My riches in glory through Christ Jesus.[8]

Let your conduct be without covetousness, My child. Be content with such things as you have. Always remember that I will never leave you nor forsake you.[9] Beloved, be anxious for nothing, but in everything by prayer and supplication, with thanksgiving, let your requests be made known to Me.[10] This will result in full contentment in your life, because My peace, which surpasses all understanding, will guard your heart and mind through Christ Jesus.[11]

All My love,

Your Abba Father

References: *(1) 1 Timothy 6:6; (2) 2 Peter 1:2; (3) 2 Peter 1:3; (4) 2 Peter 1:4; (5) Psalms 16:11; (6) Philippians 4:11; (7) Philippians 4:12-13; (8) Philippians 4:19; (9) Hebrews 13:5; (10) Philippians 4:6; (11) Philippians 4:7.*

Now you may wish to write a letter of personal response to God.

21

Correction

Key Thought: To experience God's correction is to experience His love.

Key Scripture: *"My son, do not despise the chastening of the Lord, nor be discouraged when you are rebuked by Him; for whom the Lord loves He chastens, and scourges every son whom He receives"* (Heb. 12:5-6, NKJV).

Letter From the Heart of God

My beloved child, do not be discouraged by My correction in your life; remember that I chasten you because I love you.[1] Actually, My correction in your life comes from My desire for your happiness. When you regard My reproofs of discipline, I will honor you.[2] As you heed My correction in your life, you will gain great understanding.[3]

As your ears hear and heed the words of My correction, you will learn to abide among the truly wise.[4] My child, heed My Word, and remember that all Scripture is given by My inspiration. The Bible is profitable for doctrine, for reproof, for correction, and for training in righteousness, so you will become complete and thoroughly equipped for every good work.[5]

Therefore, I beseech you to pursue righteousness, godliness, faith, love, patience, and gentleness.[6] Fight the good fight of faith, lay hold on eternal life, to which you were also called and have confessed the good confession in the presence of many witnesses.[7]

As you endure chastening, I will deal with you as My dearly beloved child. A good father must always bring correction to his child.[8] I realize that My correction in your life may not seem joyful to you. However, even though this is true, always remember that My correction will yield the peaceable fruit of righteousness in your life, as you permit yourself to be trained by it.[9] Therefore, strengthen your hands and feet. Make straight paths for your feet. Pursue peace with all people, and holiness, without which you cannot see Me.[10]

I always want what is best for you, My child. I am your loving Father; I love you with an everlasting love,[11] and I will never leave you nor forsake you.[12]

You're special to Me,

Your loving Father

References: (1) Hebrews 12:5-6; (2) Proverbs 6:23; (3) Proverbs 8:33; (4) Proverbs 3:11-12; (5) 2 Timothy 3:16; (6) Psalms 34:14; (7) 1 Timothy 6:12; (8) Hebrews 12:7; (9) Hebrews 12:11; (10) Hebrews 12:13-14; (11) Jeremiah 31:3; (12) Hebrews 13:5.

22

Deception

Key Thought: Deception involves believing lies.

Key Scripture: *"Take heed that you not be deceived"* (Luke 21:8, NKJV).

Letter From the Heart of God

My child, take heed that you be not deceived.[1] Satan is the great deceiver and the father of lies.[2] Abide in My Word. Then you shall know the truth, and the truth will make you free.[3] Remember, My loved one, that I give you My grace.

Therefore, submit yourself totally to Me. Resist the devil, and he will flee from you. Draw near to Me, and I will draw near to you.[4] In this way you will avoid deception. Be sober and vigilant, because your adversary, the devil, walks about like a roaring lion, seeking whom he may devour. Resist him, being steadfast and firm in your faith at all times.[5]

You can identify the enemy's deception, for his words will not agree with My Word, and his spirit will oppose My Spirit. Do not believe every spirit, but test the spirits, whether they are of Me, because many false prophets have gone out into the world to deceive as many as possible.[6]

By this you know My Spirit: every spirit that confesses that My Son, Jesus Christ, the Messiah, My anointed One, has come in the flesh is of Me, and every spirit that does not confess that Jesus Christ is come in the flesh is not of Me. You are My child, and you will overcome all deception, because He who lives in you is greater than he who is in the world.[7]

With all diligence, therefore, add to your faith virtue. To your virtue add knowledge. To your knowledge add self-control. To self-control, perseverance. To perseverance, godliness. To godliness, brotherly kindness. To brotherly kindness, love. For if these things are yours and they abound in your life, you will be neither barren nor unfruitful in the knowledge of your Lord Jesus Christ.[8]

Therefore, My child, be even more diligent to make your call and election sure, for if you do these things, you will never stumble into deception.[9] Be diligent to present yourself approved to Me, a worker who does not need to be ashamed, rightly dividing the word of truth.[10]

Stand fast, therefore, in the liberty by which Christ has made you free, and do not be entangled again with a yoke of bondage.[11] Walk in the Spirit, and you shall not fulfill the lust of the flesh.[12] The fruit of the Spirit is love, joy, peace, longsuffering, kindness, goodness, faithfulness, gentleness, and self-control.[13]

Be filled with the Holy Spirit.[14] Live and walk in the Holy Spirit.[15] In so doing, you will not be drawn into deception.

Grace and wisdom to you,

Your faithful Father

References: (1) Luke 2:18; (2) John 8:44; (3) John 8:31-32; (4) James 4:6-8; (5) 1 Peter 5:6-9; (6) 1 John 4:1; (7) 1 John 4:2-4; (8) 2 Peter 1:5-8; (9) 2 Peter 1:10; (10) 2 Timothy 2:15; (11) Galatians 5:1; (12) Galatians 5:16; (13) Galatians 5:22-23; (14) Ephesians 5:18; (15) Galatians 5:25.

Now you may wish to write a letter of personal response to God.

23

Deliverance

Key Thought: God's deliverance is full and complete.

Key Scripture: *"Stand fast therefore in the liberty by which Christ has made us free, and do not be entangled again with a yoke of bondage"* (Gal. 5:1, NKJV).

Letter From the Heart of God

My precious child, always remember that I am your strength, your Rock, your fortress, and your Deliverer.[1] Trust in Me, for I am your shield and the horn of your salvation.[2] When you call upon Me, I will deliver you from all your enemies.[3] I have sent angels to encamp around you and deliver you.[4]

I promise to deliver you in time of trouble, to preserve you, and to keep you alive.[5] Wait on Me. Be of good courage, and I will strengthen your heart. Wait, I say, on Me![6]

As you put your trust in Me, you will never be ashamed. I will deliver you in My righteousness, and I will cause you to escape.[7] I am your strong refuge to whom you may resort continually.[8]

Always think of Me as your help and your Deliverer.[9] Abide in My Word, and be My disciple indeed. Then you shall know the truth, and the truth will make you free.[10] When you experience the deliverance that Jesus provides, you shall be free indeed.[11]

It is My joy to proclaim liberty from captivity to you, My child. I will set you free, as you continue to look to Me for total deliverance from whatever bondage you face.[12]

In victorious love,

Your mighty Deliverer

References: (1) Psalms 18:1-2; (2) Psalms 18:2; (3) Psalms 18:3; (4) Psalms 34:7; (5) Psalms 41:1-2; (6) Psalms 27:14; (7) Psalms 71:1-2; (8) Psalms 71:3; (9) Psalms 40:17; (10) John 8:31-32; (11) John 8:36; (12) Isaiah 61:1-2.

Now you may wish to write a letter of personal response to God.

24

Depression

Key Thought: God wants to restore His joy to you.

Key Scripture: *"Out of the depths I have cried to You, O Lord; Lord, hear my voice! Let Your ears be attentive to the voice of my supplications"* (Ps. 130:1-2, NKJV).

Letter From the Heart of God

My dear child, I do hear your cry, and I am attentive to the voice of your supplications.[1] Open your heart to Me, so you can experience My joy, which is your strength.[2] Don't let your heart be troubled. Believe in My Son, Jesus, and believe in Me.[3]

Remember that your Helper, who is the Holy Spirit, will teach you all things and bring to your remembrance all the things Jesus and I have said to you.[4] My peace has been given to you through Jesus; therefore, don't let your heart be troubled, and do not be afraid.[5]

Wait upon Me, and let Me lift you up, as on the wings of an eagle, where you may soar above your circumstances, as the eagle soars above the storms that prevail on the earth.[6]

Dear one, I am love, and when you abide in love you are abiding in Me, and I am abiding in you.[7] In fact, My love has been perfected in you.[8] Because this is true, My love has the power to lift you out of your sadness and depression. Remember that there is no fear in My love.[9]

Beloved, because I love you so much, I want to remove all depression from you and restore to you the joy of your salvation.[10] I will uphold you with My generous Spirit.[11] Rejoice in Me, O righteous one, for praise from the upright is most beautiful to Me.[12] Sing a new song to Me.[13]

My eye is upon you. Continue to hope in My mercy.[14] In this way I will deliver your soul from depression.[15] Keep on waiting on Me, for I will always be your help and your shield.[16]

Enter My presence, where you will find fullness of joy and pleasures forevermore.[17] Never forget that My joy is your strength.[18]

You are precious to Me,

Your Abba Father

References: *(1) Psalms 130:1-2; (2) Nehemiah 8:10; (3) John 14:1; (4) John 14:26; (5) John 14:27; (6) Isaiah 40:31; (7) 1 John 4:16; (8) 1 John 4:17; (9) 1 John 4:18; (10) Psalms 51:12; (11) Psalms 51:12; (12) Psalms 33:1; (13) Psalms 33:3; (14) Psalms 33:18; (15) Psalms 33:19; (16) Psalms 33:20; (17) Psalms 16:11; (18) Nehemiah 8:10.*

25

Destiny

Key Thought: You are destined for great things through Christ.

Key Scripture: *"And we know that all things work together for good to those who love God, to those who are the called according to His purpose. For whom He foreknew, He also predestined to be conformed to the image of His Son, that He might be the firstborn among many brethren. Moreover whom He predestined, these He also called; whom He called, these He also justified; and whom He justified, these He also glorified"* (Rom. 8:28-30, NKJV).

Letter From the Heart of God

My dear child, I want you to realize fully that I have called you according to My purpose. Therefore, all things shall work together for good in your life. I knew you and loved you before you were born, My child, and I predestined you to be conformed to the image of My Son, so that He would be the firstborn among many brethren.[1]

You are a member of a chosen generation, a royal priesthood, a holy nation. You are one of My own special people. So, proclaim My praises, because I've called you out of darkness into My marvelous light.[2] I have already freely given you, in My Son,[3] all things that pertain to life and godliness.[4]

Dearly beloved, remember that I have blessed you with every spiritual blessing in the heavenly places in Christ.[5] I have chosen you in Him before the foundation of the world, that you should be holy and without blame before Me in love.[6] This is your destiny; indeed, I have predestined you to adoption as My child by Jesus Christ to myself according to the good pleasure of My will.[7]

Your destiny, My child, includes praising the glory of My grace by which I have made you accepted in the Beloved.[8] As a result, you have redemption through the blood of Christ and the forgiveness of your sins, according to the riches of My grace.[9]

Through My Word, I've made known to you the mystery of My will, according to My good pleasure, which I've purposed in myself, that, in the dispensation of the fullness of the times, I will gather together in one all things in Christ, both which are in heaven and which are on earth.[10]

In Christ you have obtained My inheritance, being predestined according to My purpose. Remember, My child, that I work all things according to the counsel of My will.

Because you have trusted in Christ, you will be found to the praise of My glory.[11] The Holy Spirit always bears witness with your spirit that you are My child, and, as My child, you are My heir. In fact, you are a joint heir with Christ.[12]

I know the thoughts I think about you and the plans I have for you, My child; plans to prosper you and not to harm you, plans to give you hope and a blessed future. Call upon Me and come and pray to Me, and I will listen to you and take heed to you. You will seek Me and find Me, when you seek Me with all your heart.[13]

All this is your destiny, My child.

With love and blessing,

Your heavenly Father

References: (1) Romans 8:28-29; (2) 1 Peter 2:9; (3) Romans 8:32; (4) 2 Peter 1:3; (5) Ephesians 1:3; (6) Ephesians 1:4; (7) Ephesians 1:5; (8) Ephesians 1:6; (9) Ephesians 1:7; (10) Ephesians 1:10; (11) Ephesians 1:11; (12) Romans 8:16-17; (13) Jeremiah 29:11-13.

Now you may wish to write a letter of personal response to God.

26

Diligence

Key Thought: Diligence shows your degree of devotion, dedication, and discipline.

Key Scripture: *"Keep your heart with all diligence, for out of it spring the issues of life"* (Prov. 4:23, NKJV).

Letter From the Heart of God

Dearly beloved, keep your heart with all diligence, for out of it spring the issues of life.[1] I have given you My exceedingly great and precious promises, My child, so that through these you will be a partaker of My divine nature, having escaped the corruption that is in the world through lust.[2]

For this reason, therefore, I want you to give all diligence to be sure that you add virtue to your faith and knowledge to your virtue.[3] Likewise, I want you to add self-control, perseverance, godliness, brotherly kindness, and love to your faith.[4]

The way you can do this is by being filled with the Holy Spirit,[5] who will enable you to bear His fruit in all areas of your life – love, joy, peace, longsuffering, kindness, goodness, faithfulness, gentleness, and self-control.[6]

It is so important for you to be diligent to make your call and election sure, for if you do these things you will never stumble.[7] My child, your diligence will enable you to prosper.[8] Indeed, the hand of the diligent will rule over others.[9]

Always remember that the plans of the diligent lead surely to plenty.[10] I want you to keep My precepts diligently.[11] This will always result in great blessing in your life. When you diligently seek My face you will surely find Me.[12]

My child, keep My words, and treasure My commands within you. Keep My commands and live, and My law as the apple of your eye. Bind them on your fingers; write them on the tablet of your heart.[13]

Through such diligence you will receive many blessings, for I reward all those who diligently seek Me.[14]

With all My love,

Your Father in heaven

References: *(1) Proverbs 4:23; (2) 2 Peter 1:4; (3) 2 Peter 1:5; (4) 2 Peter 1:6; (5) Ephesians 5:18; (6) Galatians 5:22-23; (7) 2 Peter 1:10; (8) Proverbs 10:4; (9) Proverbs 12:24; (10) Proverbs 21:5; (11) Psalms 119:4; (12) Psalms 27:8; (13) Proverbs 7:1-3; (14) Hebrews 11:6.*

27

Discouragement

Key Thought: Encourage your heart in God.

Key Scripture: *"Look, the Lord your God has set the land before you; go up and possess it, as the Lord God of your fathers has spoken to you; do not fear or be discouraged"* (Deut. 1:21, NKJV).

Letter From the Heart of God

My precious child, I never want you to be discouraged. Possess the land I've given you, and don't allow fear or discouragement to come against you.[1] Be strong and of good courage, for the inheritance I've promised is yours.[2] Be strong and very courageous.[3]

Meditate on and delight in My Word. Then you will be like a fruitful tree planted by the rivers of water and whatever you do will prosper.[4] Do not let My Word depart from your mouth, but meditate in it day and night, that you may observe to do according to all that is written in it. For then you will make your way prosperous, and then you will have good success.[5] Do not be afraid or dismayed, for I am always with you wherever you go.[6]

The opposite of discouragement is encouragement, and both words come from the word "courage." My child, I want you to be like David who learned to encourage himself in Me. As he did this, he gained great strength.[7]

Bless Me at all times, and let My praise be in your mouth continually.[8] Let your soul make its boast in Me.[9] Magnify Me, and exalt My name.[10] Seek Me, and I will deliver you.[11] Look to Me, and I will make you radiant.[12]

Do not be worried or anxious about anything. Bring your concerns to Me in prayer, with thanksgiving, and I will give you a peace that is beyond understanding that will enable you to wait patiently for the answer. Remember, thanksgiving and prayer are important keys in overcoming discouragement.[13]

Be encouraged, My child, for those who seek Me will never suffer want or deprivation of any kind.[14] As you meditate on these truths and believe them, the discouragement you're experiencing will leave you, I promise.

With much love,

Your faithful Father

References: *(1) Deuteronomy 1:21; (2) Joshua 1:6; (3) Joshua 1:7; (4) Psalms 1:1-3; (5) Joshua 1:8; (6) Joshua 1:9; (7) 1 Samuel 30:6; (8) Psalms 34:1; (9) Psalms 34:2; (10) Psalms 34:3; (11) Psalms 34:4; (12) Psalms 34:5; (13) Philippians 4:6-7; (14) Psalms 34:10.*

28

Earnestness

Key Thought: Earnestness is an avenue to great blessing in your life.

Key Scripture: *"Therefore we must give the more earnest heed to the things we have heard, lest we drift away"* (Heb. 2:1, NKJV).

Letter From the Heart of God

My dearly loved child, give earnest heed to My Word, so you will never drift away.[1] Remember that all My promises are yes in Christ, and in Him amen.[2]

I have established you in Christ, and I have anointed you.[3] I have also sealed you and given you the Holy Spirit in your heart as a guarantee.[4] Therefore, I ask you to be earnest in your devotion to Me.

Remember that I give you the victory through your Lord Jesus Christ.[5] Therefore, I want you to be earnestly steadfast, unmovable, always abounding in My work, knowing that your labor is never in vain in Me.[6] Be earnest as you do My work, My child, realizing that you are a fellow worker with Me.[7]

Therefore, beloved one, look forward to all that I will bring to pass. Be diligent, that I may always find you to be living in a state of peace and confidence before Me, without spot and blameless.[8] This is the earnest devotion I seek from you, My precious child.

If you abide in Christ, and let His words abide in you, you will ask what you desire, and it shall be done for you.[9] Your earnestness in prayer will glorify and please Me, and it will lead you to bear much fruit.[10] Do not lose heart, My child, because your inward being is constantly being renewed day by day.[11]

Walk by faith and not by sight.[12] Earnestly serve Me. I dwell in you and walk with you. I am your God, and you are My child.[13] Fight the good fight of faith. Take hold of the eternal life to which you were called.[14]

I love you, My child.

Faithfully,

Your loving Father

References: (1) Hebrews 2:1; (2) 2 Corinthians 1:20; (3) 2 Corinthians 1:21; (4) 2 Corinthians 1:22; (5) 1 Corinthians 15:57; (6) 1 Corinthians 15:58; (7) 1 Corinthians 3:9; (8) 2 Peter 3:14; (9) John 15:7; (10) John 15:8; (11) 2 Corinthians 4:16; (12) 2 Corinthians 5:7; (13) 2 Corinthians 6:16; (14) 1 Timothy 6:12.

Now you may wish to write a letter of personal response to God.

29

Edification

Key Thought: To be edified is to be built up and strengthened.

Key Scripture: *"Speaking the truth in love, may grow up in all things into Him who is the head – Christ – from whom the whole body, joined and knit together by what every joint supplies, according to the effective working by which every part does its share, causes growth of the body for the edifying of itself in love"* (Eph. 4:15-16, NKJV).

Letter 'From the Heart of God

My dearly loved child, speak the truth in love at all times, so that you will grow up in all things into Christ, for He is the head of the Body, His church. It is love that will bring the edification you seek.[1] Always remember that knowledge puffs up, but love will edify you.[2]

My kingdom does not consist of eating and drinking, but of righteousness and peace and joy in the Holy Spirit.[3] Therefore, I want you to pursue the things which make for peace and the things by which you may edify others.[4]

Be zealous for spiritual gifts, that you may edify your fellow-believers.[5] Let everything you do be done for edification of yourself and others.[6] Give no heed to fables and endless genealogies, which cause disputes; rather, give your attention to godly edification, which is in faith.[7]

Now the purpose of the commandment is love from a pure heart, from a good conscience, and from sincere faith.[8] These things will edify and strengthen you, My child.

Let no corrupt or unwholesome word proceed out of your mouth, but only those words that are good for edification and minister grace to those who hear what you are saying.[9] Do not grieve the Holy Spirit by whom you were sealed for the day of redemption.[10]

Let all bitterness, wrath, anger, clamor, and evil speaking be put away from you, with all malice.[11] And be kind to others, tenderhearted and forgiving, even as I have forgiven you in Christ.[12] This, My child, will edify you and bring edification to others.

Peace, love, and joy,

Your mighty God

References: (1) Ephesians 4:15-16; (2) 1 Corinthians 8:1; (3) Romans 14:17; (4) Romans 14:19; (5) 1 Corinthians 14:12; (6) 1 Corinthians 14:26; (7) 1 Timothy 1:4; (8) 1 Timothy 1:5; (9) Ephesians 4:29; (10) Ephesians 4:30; (11) Ephesians 4:31; (12) Ephesians 4:32.

30

Endurance

Key Thought: To endure you must keep on keeping on.

Key Scripture: *"For you have need of endurance, so that after you have done the will of God, you may receive the promise"* (Heb. 10:36, NKJV).

Letter From the Heart of God

My special child, you do need to endure, so that, after you have done My will, you will be able to receive My promises.[1] Therefore, I encourage you to lay aside every weight and the sin which so easily besets you, so you will be able to run with endurance the race I have set before you.[2] Keep looking unto Jesus, who is the Author and Finisher of your faith. Remember that He endured the cross for you, and He is now sitting at My right hand here in heaven.[3]

My child, you must endure hardness as a good soldier of Jesus Christ.[4] You will be blessed as you learn to endure.[5] Indeed, I want you to know that, by enduring temptation, you will find yourself approved, and you shall receive the crown of life, which I've promised to all who love Me.[6]

It is love that will enable you to endure, My beloved. Always remember that love suffers long and is kind. Love does not envy. Love does not parade itself, and it is not puffed up.[7] Love does not behave rudely, does not seek its own, is not easily provoked, thinks no evil.[8] Love does not rejoice in iniquity, but rejoices in the truth.[9] Indeed, love bears all things, believes all things, hopes all things, and endures all things.[10]

My child, I am a rewarder of those who diligently seek me.[11] Keep on keeping on, and keep on seeking Me, and I promise that you will be rewarded.

Eternal love,

Your everlasting Father

References: *(1) Hebrews 10:36; (2) Hebrews 12:1; (3) Hebrews 12:2; (4) 2 Timothy 2:3; (5) James 5:11; (6) James 1:12; (7) 1 Corinthians 13:4; (8) 1 Corinthians 13:5; (9) 1 Corinthians 13:6; (10) 1 Corinthians 13:7; (11) Hebrews 11:6.*

Now you may wish to write a letter of personal response to God.

31

Envy

Key Thought: Envy opens the door to many problems.

Key Scripture: *"Let us walk properly, as in the day, not in revelry and drunkenness, not in lewdness and lust, not in strife and envy. But put on the Lord Jesus Christ, and make no provision for the flesh, to fulfill its lusts"* (Rom. 13:13-14, NKJV).

Letter From the Heart of God

Dear one, always walk properly, and never walk in strife and envy. The way you will be able to do this is by putting on the Lord Jesus Christ, and making no provision for the flesh, to fulfill its lusts.[1]

As you know, envy comes from a carnal mind. It is one of the works of the flesh, which include envy, adultery, fornication, uncleanness, lewdness, idolatry, sorcery, hatred, contentions, jealousies, outbursts of wrath, selfish ambitions, dissensions, heresies, murders, drunkenness, revelries, and the like.[2]

Where envy and strife exist, there is confusion and every evil work of the enemy.[3] I have translated you out of the power of darkness, into the kingdom of the Son of My love, Jesus Christ.[4] Therefore, give no place to the devil, for envy lets him in.[5]

My child, I do not want you to fall victim to any of these things. Therefore, be continually filled with the Holy Spirit.[6] Remember that the fruit of the Spirit is love, joy, peace, longsuffering, kindness, goodness, faithfulness, gentleness, and self-control.[7] If you live in the Spirit, be sure also to walk in the Spirit, and you will be free from envy.[8]

Never forget that the law of the Spirit of life in Christ Jesus has made you free from the law of sin and death.[9] Those who live according to the flesh set their minds on the things of the flesh, but I want you to set your mind on the things of the Spirit, as you endeavor to live according to the Spirit.[10]

As I mentioned above, envy comes from a carnal mind, and a carnal mind leads to death. When you are spiritually minded, My child, you will experience life and peace.[11] Because this is true, I want you to resist all temptations to envy. Remember that the carnal mind is enmity against Me, because it is not subject to My law and never can be.[12]

When you envy, therefore, you cannot please Me.[13] Why is that? Because, if you will trust Me, I am able to give you everything you need.[14] Envy says you don't trust Me to take care of you.

Allow yourself to be led by My Spirit,[15] remembering that you did not receive the spirit of bondage again to any kind of fear. You need not fear lack or that I am unable to meet your needs and give you the legitimate desires of your heart.[16]

You have received the Spirit of adoption by whom you are able to cry out, "Abba Father."[17] When you do that, know that I will hear and answer.[18]

Grace and peace to you,

Your loving Father

References: (1) Romans 13:13-14; (2) Galatians 5:19-20; (3) James 3:16; (4) Colossians 1:13; (5) Ephesians 4:27; (6) Ephesians 5:18; (7) Galatians 5:22-23; (8) Galatians 5:25; (9) Romans 8:2; (10) Romans 8:5; (11) Romans 8:6; (12) Romans 8:7; (13) Romans 8:8; (14) Philippians 4:19; (15) Romans 8:14; (16) Psalms 37:4; (17) Romans 8:15; (18) Jeremiah 33:3.

Now you may wish to write a letter of personal response to God.

32

Eternity

Key Thought: Eternity begins now.

Key Scripture: *"In My Father's house are many mansions; if it were not so, I would have told you. I go to prepare a place for you. And if I go and prepare a place for you, I will come again and receive you to Myself; that where I am, there you may be also"* (John 14:2-3, NKJV).

Letter From the Heart of God

My precious child, I love you. As Jesus explained, there are many mansions in My house, and He has prepared a place for you to enjoy for all eternity. Jesus will come again, and He will receive you to himself, so that you can spend eternity with Him and Me.[1]

Though I cannot tell you exactly when Jesus will return for you,[2] I want you to take heart in the realization that, because I have loved you so much, I sent My only begotten Son to die for you, so you would not perish but have everlasting life.[3]

Most assuredly, therefore, I say to you that, because you have heard My Word and you have believed in Jesus and in Me, you already have eternal life.[4] Because you know

Me and My Son, Jesus Christ, you do have everlasting life.[5]

Therefore, My child, I want you to pursue righteousness, godliness, faith, love, patience, and gentleness.[6] Fight the good fight of faith as you take hold of the eternal life to which I have called you.[7]

Do not look at the things which are seen, but at the things which are not seen. For the things which are seen are temporary, but the things which are not seen are eternal.[8] Walk by faith, and not by sight.[9]

Make it your aim to please Me,[10] remembering that to be absent from the body is to be present with Me for eternity.[11] Surely goodness and mercy will follow you all the days of your life, and you will dwell in My house forever.[12]

Always and forever,

Your unchanging Father

References: *(1) John 14:1-3; (2) Acts 1:7; (3) John 3:16; (4) John 5:24; (5) John 17:3; (6) 1 Timothy 6:11; (7) 1 Timothy 6:12; (8) 2 Corinthians 4:18; (9) 2 Corinthians 5:7; (10) 2 Corinthians 5:9; (11) 2 Corinthians 5:8; (12) Psalms 23:6.*

Now you may wish to write a letter of personal response to God.

33
Faith

Key Thought: Faith is your key to victory.

Key Scripture: *"The only thing that counts is faith expressing itself through love"* (Gal. 5:6, NIV).

Letter From the Heart of God

My child, hold on to the truth that the only thing that really counts is faith expressing itself through love.[1] It is important for you to realize that faith comes through hearing, and the hearing that builds your faith is hearing My Word.[2]

Without faith it is impossible to please Me, for when you come to Me you must believe that I am, and that I am a Rewarder of all those who diligently seek Me.[3]

Let Me define faith for you, My child. It is the substance of things hoped for, the evidence of things not seen.[4] Those whom I have justified shall live by faith,[5] and I have called you to walk by faith and not by sight.[6]

My precious child, never forget that faith is the victory that overcomes the world.[7] I will reward your faith. Indeed, whatever things you ask in prayer, believing, you will receive.[8] Therefore, keep on fighting the good fight of faith, and take hold of the eternal life to which I have called you.[9]

My child, I want you to be like My servant Abraham, who did not waver at My promise through unbelief, but was strong in faith, giving glory to Me, being fully convinced that what I had promised, I was willing and able to perform.[10]

You can be certain, My child, that when you finish the race, after fighting the good fight and keeping the faith, I will reward you with the crown of righteousness.[11]

With much love,

Your faithful Father

References: *(1) Galatians 5:6; (2) Romans 10:17; (3) Hebrews 11:6; (4) Hebrews 11:1; (5) Habakkuk 2:4; (6) 2 Corinthians 5:7; (7) 1 John 5:4; (8) Matthew 21:22; (9) 1 Timothy 6:12; (10) Romans 4:20; (11) 2 Timothy 4:7-8.*

Now you may wish to write a letter of personal response to God.

34

Faithfulness of God

Key Thought: God is always faithful.

Key Scripture: *"Through the Lord's mercies we are not consumed, because His compassions fail not. They are new every morning; great is Your faithfulness"* (Lam. 3:22-23, NKJV).

Letter From the Heart of God

My dear child, I want you to know that I will be faithful to you always.[1] I am not a man that I should lie. What I have said, I will do. What I have spoken, I shall make good.[2] My Word, that goes forth out of My mouth, will not return unto Me void but will accomplish My pleasure and prosper in the purpose to which I send it.[3]

Trust in Me with all your heart and do not lean unto your own understanding. In all your ways acknowledge Me, and I promise I will direct your paths.[4] Draw near to Me with a true heart in full assurance of faith.[5] Hold fast the confession of your hope without wavering, for I will be faithful to fulfill all My promises to you.[6]

In My faithfulness I've called you into fellowship with My Son, Jesus Christ.[7] Trust in Him and in Me, and do good. Dwell in the land, and feed on My faithfulness.[8] Delight yourself in Me, and I will give you the desires of your heart.[9] Commit your way to Me, trust also in Me, and I promise to bring it to pass.[10]

All of My promises are yes in Christ and in Him amen.[11] I have established you in Christ, and I have anointed you.[12] I, your God, have sealed you and given you the Spirit in your heart as a guarantee.[13]

Never forget, My child, that I am able to do exceeding abundantly beyond all that you can ask or think, according to the power of the Holy Spirit who is at work in you.[14]

Faithfully,

Your heavenly Father

References: *(1) Lamentations 3:22-23; (2) Numbers 23:19; (3) Isaiah 55:11; (4) Proverbs 3:5-6; (5) Hebrews 10:22; (6) Hebrews 10:23; (7) 1 Corinthians 1:9; (8) Psalms 37:3; (9) Psalms 37:4; (10) Psalms 37:5; (11) 2 Corinthians 1:20; (12) 2 Corinthians 1:21; (13) 2 Corinthians 5:5; (14) Ephesians 3:20.*

Now you may wish to write a letter of personal response to God.

35

Fear

Key Thought: Love is the antidote for fear.

Key Scripture: *"For God hath not given us the spirit of fear; but of power, and of love, and of a sound mind"* (2 Tim. 1:7).

Letter From the Heart of God

My dear child, I love you and I never want you to live in fear. There is no fear in My love; indeed, My perfect love casts out all fear from your life.[1] I have not given you a spirit of fear, but I have given you a spirit of power and of love and of a sound mind.[2]

You have not received the spirit of bondage again to fear, but you have received the Spirit of adoption by whom you are able to cry out, "Abba Father."[3] You are Mine, and I love you with a perfect love. Receive My love now, and let it cast out all fear from you.[4]

My child, please remember that the fear of man always brings a snare with it. I want you to trust in Me, for I will keep you safe.[5] I will never leave you nor forsake you, therefore you may boldly say, "God himself is my helper; I will not be afraid. What can man do to me?"[6] Be strong and of good courage; do not be afraid, nor dismayed, for I am with you everywhere and at all times.[7]

Never forget that I am your light and your salvation. I am the strength of your life. Therefore, you need not fear anyone or anything.[8] Let not your heart be troubled; neither let it be afraid.[9] I am your refuge and your fortress. I am your God, and I want you to place all your trust in Me.[10]

Because you have set your love upon Me, I will deliver you, and when you call upon Me I will answer you.[11] I will give My angels charge over you, to keep you in all your ways.[12]

I promise that no weapon formed against you will prosper, for this is your heritage as My child.[13] Remember, you are more than a conqueror through Christ. Be fully persuaded that nothing shall ever be able to separate you from My love.[14]

If I am for you, who can ever be successful against you?[15] Do not fear, My beloved, for it is My good pleasure to give you the kingdom.[16]

In perfect love,

Your Abba Father

References: (1) 1 John 4:18; (2) 2 Timothy 1:7; (3) Romans 8:15; (4) 1 John 4:18; (5) Proverbs 29:25; (6) Hebrews 13:5-6; (7) Joshua 1:9; (8) Psalms 27:1; (9) John 14:1; (10) Psalms 91:2; (11) Psalms 91:14-15; (12) Psalms 91:11; (13) Isaiah 54:17; (14) Romans 8:37-39; (15) Romans 8:31; (16) Luke 12:32.

36

Freedom

Key Thought: You are free indeed!

Key Scripture: *"Then Jesus said to those Jews who believed Him, 'If you abide in My word, you are My disciples indeed. And you shall know the truth, and the truth shall make you free'"* (John 8:31-32, NKJV).

Letter From the Heart of God

Dearly loved child, I want you to experience the full freedom that all of My children are entitled to. Therefore, abide in My Word and be a true disciple. Then you shall know the truth, and the truth shall make you free.[1] Remember, if Jesus makes you free, you are free indeed.[2]

It is your responsibility, My child, to stand fast in the liberty wherewith Christ has made you free, and not to become entangled again with a yoke of bondage.[3]

I sent Jesus to proclaim liberty to the captives, and to set the prisoners free.[4] I sent Him to comfort all who mourn, and to console those who mourn in Zion. I give you beauty instead of ashes, the oil of joy for your mourning, and the garment of praise for the spirit of heaviness, so that you may be called a tree of righteousness.[5]

This is the glorious liberty I've reserved for all My children.[6] My precious child, I called you to liberty. Only do not use your freedom as an opportunity for the flesh, but, through love, serve others.[7] Always remember that where the Holy Spirit is there is liberty.[8] Walk in the Spirit and you will not fulfill the lusts of the flesh.[9]

The law of the Spirit of life in Christ Jesus has made you free from the law of sin and death.[10] Enjoy the freedom I've given to you, My child.

Love and freedom,

Your heavenly Father

References: *(1) John 8:31-32; (2) John 8:36; (3) Galatians 5:1; (4) Isaiah 61:1; (5) Isaiah 61:2-3; (6) Romans 8:21; (7) Galatians 5:13; (8) 2 Corinthians 3:17; (9) Galatians 5:16; (10) Romans 8:2.*

Now you may wish to write a letter of personal response to God.

37

Godliness

Key Thought: Godliness is a quality that is directly related to our nearness to God.

Key Scripture: *"Bodily exercise profiteth little: but godliness is profitable unto all things"* (1 Tim. 4:8).

Letter From the Heart of God

My lovely child, as you draw near to Me, I promise to draw near to you.[1] In this drawing close to Me you will discover that godliness will become a natural part of your life, and you will learn that godliness is profitable in all things.[2]

My power has given to you all things that pertain to life and godliness, and you will increase in godliness, as you get to know Me better.[3] My promises are for you, My child, and these exceedingly great and precious promises will enable you to partake of My divine nature.[4] Thus will you have godliness in your life.

Therefore, sow to the Spirit, for of the Spirit you shall reap a harvest of eternal life and the godliness that comes with it.[5] Remember that godliness in your life, with contentment, is always great gain for you.[6]

I want you to be happy, My child, and you can be sure that godliness in your life will lead you to greater happiness.[7] Though many may feel that the mystery of godliness is great,[8] you are learning that, by seeking Me and My righteousness, everything else will be provided.[9]

Because you have been born again, you are able to overcome the world.[10] You are an overcomer, My child. Remember that I have no greater joy than to hear that My children walk in truth.[11] Therefore, keep yourself in My love, and look for the mercy of your Lord Jesus Christ.[12]

All My love,

God, your Father

References: *(1) James 4:8; (2) 1 Timothy 4:8; (3) 2 Peter 1:3; (4) 2 Peter 1:4; (5) Galatians 6:8; (6) 1 Timothy 6:6; (7) Psalms 144:15; (8) 1 Timothy 3:16; (9) Matthew 6:33; (10) 1 John 5:4; (11) 3 John 4; (12) Jude 21.*

Now you may wish to write a letter of personal response to God.

38

God's Word

Key Thought: God's Word reveals God's will for your life.

Key Scripture: *"For the word of God is living and powerful, and sharper than any two-edged sword, piercing even to the division of soul and spirit, and of joints and marrow, and is a discerner of the thoughts and intents of the heart"* (Heb. 4:12, NKJV).

Letter From the Heart of God

Dearly beloved child, take heed to My Word. Realize that it is alive, and it is powerful. It will pierce even to the division of your soul and spirit, and it will discern the thoughts and intents of your heart.[1] Hide My Word in your heart, My child, for it will keep you from sin.[2]

My Word will guard you from temptation,[3] because it is the sword of the Spirit, and it is your effective weapon in warfare against the enemy.[4] It will guide your steps, for it is a lamp unto your feet and a light unto your path.[5]

As you hear My Word, it will build your faith.[6] My child, meditate in My Word faithfully, and do according to all that is written in it. Then you will prosper and have good success.[7] In doing so, you will be like a fruitful tree planted by the rivers of water,[8] for My Word is life to you and brings health to all your flesh.[9]

Remember, My child, that My Word is near you; it is in your mouth and in your heart. It is the Word of faith,[10] the incorruptible seed, which lives and abides forever, by which you were born again.[11] My Word is very good indeed.[12] Hope in My Word.[13]

My Word is truth,[14] and knowing its truth will make you free.[15] As a newborn babe, continue to desire the sincere milk of My Word, for by it you will keep on growing.[16]

In love and truth,

Your Father God

References: *(1) Hebrews 4:12; (2) Psalms 119:9-11; (3) Luke 4:4; (4) Ephesians 6:17; (5) Psalms 119:105; (6) Romans 10:17; (7) Joshua 1:8; (8) Psalms 1:3; (9) Proverbs 4:20-22; (10) Romans 10:8-9; (11) 1 Peter 1:23; (12) 2 Kings 20:19; (13) Psalms 130:5; (14) John 17:17; (15) John 8:32; (16) 1 Peter 2:2.*

Now you may wish to write a letter of personal response to God.

39

Gospel of Jesus Christ

Key Thought: The Gospel of Jesus Christ is the greatest news the world has ever heard.

Key Scripture: *"For I am not ashamed of the gospel of Christ, for it is the power of God to salvation for everyone who believes, for the Jew first and also for the Greek"* (Rom. 1:16, NKJV).

Letter From the Heart of God

My dear one, never be ashamed of the Gospel of Jesus Christ, for I tell you, truly, it contains My power unto salvation for all who believe its truth.[1] My call to all mankind is to repent and believe the good news of the gospel.[2]

Never forget the truth that Jesus expressed, "Whosoever shall lose his life for My sake and the gospel's, the same shall save it."[3]

Let this truth come to full fruition in your life, My child, and wherever you go throughout the world, preach the Gospel of Jesus Christ.[4] How shall people hear without a preacher?[5] How beautiful are the feet of those who preach the gospel![6]

In Christ Jesus I have begotten you through the gospel.[7] Set yourself, therefore, for the defense of the Gospel of Jesus Christ.[8]

Do not let yourself ever be moved away from the hope of the gospel.[9] Remember, My child, My Word is not bound or limited.[10] I will hasten to perform My Word,[11] and it will always accomplish the purposes for which I send it.[12]

Preach the Word! Be ready in season and out of season. Convince, rebuke, exhort, with all longsuffering and teaching.[13]

As you go forth to proclaim the gospel, you will find it an exciting adventure to be led by My Spirit,[14] who will guide you into all truth[15] and bring to your remembrance all things that I have taught you.[16]

Love and blessings,

Your heavenly Father

References: *(1) Romans 1:16; (2) Mark 1:15; (3) Mark 8:35; (4) Mark 16:15; (5) Romans 10:14; (6) Romans 10:15; (7) 1 Corinthians 4:15; (8) Philippians 1:17; (9) Colossians 1:23; (10) 2 Timothy 2:9; (11) Jeremiah 1:12; (12) Isaiah 55:11; (13) 2 Timothy 4:2; (14) Romans 8:14; (15) John 16:13; (16) John 14:26.*

Now you may wish to write a letter of personal response to God.

40

Grace

Key Thought: God's grace is a gift to you.

Key Scripture: *"For by grace you have been saved through faith, and that not of yourselves; it is the gift of God, not of works, lest anyone should boast"* (Eph. 2:8-9, NKJV).

Letter From the Heart of God

My dear child, it is always a joy for Me to impart My grace to you by the effective working of My power in your life.[1] Grace is My personal gift to you,[2] and it enables you to be who you could not be,[3] to do what you could not do,[4] to believe what you could not believe,[5] and to receive what you could not receive.[6] It is by My grace that you have been saved through faith.[7]

I want you to realize that My grace is always sufficient for you, and My strength is made perfect in your times of weakness.[8] Accept My invitation to come boldly to My throne of grace, that you may obtain mercy and find grace to help in any time of need.[9] I am always there, waiting to help you, because I love you.[10]

You have been justified by faith and have peace with Me through your Lord Jesus

Christ Through Him, you have access into My grace in which you stand. So, rejoice in the hope of My glory.[11] The law of the Spirit of life in Christ Jesus has set you free from the law of sin and death.[12] Therefore, stand fast in the liberty wherewith Christ has set you free and do not allow yourself to be entangled with any yoke of bondage.[13]

I want to give you even more grace.[14] Therefore, submit your life totally to Me. Resist the devil, and he will flee from you.[15] Draw near to Me, and I will draw near to you. Cleanse your hands and purify your heart.[16]

Humble yourself in My sight, and I promise to lift you up.[17] Call unto me, and I will answer you and show you great and mighty things, which you do not know.[18] Grace and peace to you, My child.[19]

With all My love,

Your Abba Father

References: (1) Ephesians 3:7; (2) 2 Corinthians 9:14-15; (3) 2 Corinthians 5:17; (4) Philippians 4:13; (5) Romans 10:17; (6) Mark 11:24; (7) Ephesians 2:8-9; (8) 2 Corinthians 12:9; (9) Hebrews 4:16; (10) 1 John 4:8; (11) Romans 5:1-2; (12) Romans 8:2; (13) Galatians 5:1; (14) James 4:6; (15) James 4:7; (16) James 4:8; (17) James 4:10; (18) Jeremiah 33:3; (19) Romans 1:7.

41

Grief and Mourning

Key Thought: In your grief remember that God is near.

Key Scripture: *"The Lord is near to those who have a broken heart, and saves such as have a contrite spirit"* (Ps. 34:18, NKJV).

Letter From the Heart of God

Dearly beloved, I am near to you.[1] Pour out your heart before Me, remembering that I am your refuge.[2] Because I love you, I give you beauty for ashes and the oil of joy for your mourning. I place upon you the garment of praise for your spirit of heaviness.[3] Receive My comfort,[4] as you remember that I am the Father of mercies and the God of all comfort.[5]

I, even I, am He who is with you to comfort you now.[6] As a mother comforts her children, I comfort you.[7] I have promised to bless and comfort you in your time of mourning.[8] So, remember not to grieve as those who have no hope.[9]

Even when you walk through the valley of the shadow of death, you need not fear any evil, because I am always with you.[10] My rod and My staff will bring comfort to you.[11] I have prepared a table before you in the presence of your enemies. I have anointed your head with oil, and your cup overflows.[12]

Surely goodness and mercy shall follow you all the days of your life, and you will dwell in My house forever.[13] Come, spend time with Me, My beloved, for I heal the broken-hearted[14] and in My presence there is fullness of joy.[15]

I care for you,

Your heavenly Father

References: (1) Psalms 34:18; (2) Psalms 62:8; (3) Isaiah 61:3; (4) Jeremiah 31:13; (5) 2 Corinthians 1:3; (6) Isaiah 51:12; (7) Isaiah 66:13; (8) Matthew 5:4; (9) 1 Thessalonians 4:13; (10) Psalms 23:4; (11) Psalms 23:4; (12) Psalms 23:5; (13) Psalms 23:6; (14) Isaiah 61:1; (15) Psalms 16:11.

Now you may wish to write a letter of personal response to God.

42

Guidance

Key Thought: God will guide you each step of the way.

Key Scripture: *"Trust in the Lord with all your heart, and lean not on your own understanding; in all your ways acknowledge Him, and He shall direct your paths"* (Prov. 3:5-6, NKJV).

Letter From the Heart of God

My precious child, trust Me with all your heart, and do not lean on your own understanding. Instead, in all your ways I want you to acknowledge Me, and, if you do this, I promise to direct your steps.[1]

Remember that My Word is a lamp unto your feet and a light unto your path.[2] It will give you the guidance you need. Let Me be your eyes.[3] Let Me be your lamp[4] and let Me guide you with My eye.[5] It is I who makes you to lie down in green pastures and leads you beside the still waters. I will restore your soul.[6]

I promise to show you My ways and to teach you My paths.[7] Your steps are ordered by Me, and I delight to see you following My paths.[8] My light and My truth will lead you.[9] I promise to be your God forever and ever. I will be your Guide even unto death.[10]

Jesus is the way, the truth, and the life, and it is through Him that you may come to Me for the guidance you seek.[11] Let the word of Christ dwell in you richly in all wisdom.[12]

You are My temple, for My Spirit dwells in you.[13] He gives quickening life to your body[14] and He bears witness with your spirit that you are My child.[15] He will guide you into all truth,[16] for He is the Spirit of truth.[17] Be continually filled afresh with the Holy Spirit,[18] who will give you wisdom and revelation in the knowledge of Me and enlighten the eyes of your understanding.[19]

Whatever you do in word or deed, do all in the name of the Lord Jesus, giving thanks to Me through Him.[20]

Grace and peace to you, My child.[21]

Your heavenly Guide,

Father God

References: *(1) Proverbs 3:5-6; (2) Psalms 119:105; (3) Numbers 10:31; (4) 2 Samuel 22:29; (5) Psalms 32:8; (6) Psalms 23:2-3; (7) Psalms 25:4; (8) Psalms 37:23; (9) Psalms 43:3; (10) Psalms 48:14; (11) John 14:6; (12) Colossians 3:16; (13) 1 Corinthians 3:16; (14) Romans 8:11; (15) Romans 8:16; (16) John 16:13; (17) John 14:17; (18) Ephesians 5:18; (19) Ephesians 1:17-18; (20) Colossians 3:17; (21) Ephesians 1:2.*

Now you may wish to write a letter of personal response to God.

43

Guilt

Key Thought: The blood of Jesus Christ cleanses you from all sin.

Key Scripture: *"There is therefore now no condemnation to those who are in Christ Jesus, who do not walk according to the flesh, but according to the Spirit. For the law of the Spirit of life in Christ Jesus has made me free from the law of sin and death"* (Rom. 8:1-2, NKJV).

Letter From the Heart of God

My child, do not forget that there is no need ever to feel condemnation, when you are in Christ Jesus. Do not walk according to the flesh any longer, but walk according to the Spirit, for the law of the Spirit of life in Christ Jesus has made you free from the law of sin and death.[1]

The blood of Jesus Christ, My Son, cleanses you from all unrighteousness, when you walk in the light as He is in the light.[2] When you confess your sins to Me, I promise to be faithful and just to forgive you of your sins and to cleanse you from all unrighteousness.[3]

If you try to cover your sins, you cannot prosper; but, if you confess and forsake your sins, you will receive My mercy.[4] By following these guidelines, you will never need to live in guilt or condemnation again. For Christ's sake I have forgiven you.[5]

You have redemption through Jesus' blood, even the forgiveness of your sins.[6] Your sins are forgiven you for His name's sake.[7]

According to My abundant mercy I have begotten you again to a living hope through the Resurrection of Jesus Christ from the dead.[8] I have given you an incorruptible and undefiled inheritance that does not fade away, and I've reserved it in heaven for you.[9] I promise to keep you by My power.[10]

For all these reasons, I want you to put all guilt and condemnation behind you. When you have done that, you will have confidence before Me; and, whatever you ask, you will receive from Me, because you have obeyed My Word and done what is pleasing to Me.[11]

Therefore, forgetting those things which are behind you, reach forward to those things which lie ahead and press toward the goal for the prize of My upward call in Christ Jesus.[12]

Much love and peace,

Your forgiving heavenly Father

References: (1) Romans 8:1-2; (2) 1 John 1:7; (3) 1 John 1:9; (4) Proverbs 28:13; (5) Ephesians 4:32; (6) Colossians 1:14; (7) 1 John 2:12; (8) 1 Peter 1:3; (9) 1 Peter 1:4, (10) 1 Peter 1:5; (11) 1 John 3:21-23; (12) Philippians 3:13-14.

44

Healing

Key Thought: All healing comes from God.

Key Scripture: *"Bless the Lord, O my soul, and forget not all His benefits: who forgives all your iniquities, who heals all your diseases"* (Ps. 103:2-3, NKJV).

Letter From the Heart of God

My child, don't forget all of My benefits. I forgive all your iniquities and I heal all your diseases.[1] Indeed, I desire that you may prosper in all things and be in health just as your soul prospers.[2] As you serve Me, I will bless your food and drink, and I will remove sickness from your midst.[3]

All healing comes from Me, for I am the Lord, your God, who heals you.[4] As you need healing, My child, ask Me for it, and I will heal you.[5] I will restore health to you and heal you of all your wounds.[6]

I promise to supply all of your needs, including healing, by My riches in glory through Christ Jesus.[7] I have provided an open door of healing for you through the stripes of Jesus,[8] and by His stripes you were healed.[9] He is the same yesterday, today, and forever.[10]

My child, give your full attention to My words, and hear My sayings.[11] I have sent My Word to heal you and deliver you.[12] My Word is alive and powerful.[13] Do not let My words depart from before your eyes. Keep them in the midst of your heart, for they are life to you and health to all your flesh.[14]

Guard your heart with all diligence, for out of it spring the issues of life.[15] Remember, My child, a merry heart does you good like a medicine.[16]

I want you to keep on remembering that all My promises are yes and amen in Christ Jesus.[17] I am able to do exceedingly abundantly above all that you can ask or think, according to My power which is at work within you.[18] Indeed, all things are possible with Me.[19]

So, be an imitator of them who through faith and patience inherit My promises.[20] Be strong in faith, giving glory to Me, and be fully persuaded that, what I have promised, I am able and willing to perform in your life.[21] I love you, and I am ready to perform My Word in your behalf.[22]

Always remember that faith to believe comes from hearing My Word.[23] Have faith in Me[24] and do not doubt in your heart.[25] When you desire healing, believe that you receive it when you pray, and you shall have it.[26]

Ask, and it will be given to you; seek, and you will find; knock, and it will be opened to you. For everyone who asks receives, and the one who seeks finds, and to everyone who knocks it will be opened.[27]

Whatever you ask Me in the name of Jesus, I will give it to you. Therefore, ask and receive, that your joy may be full.[28] I am the God of hope, and I will fill you with all joy and peace, as you believe, that you may abound in hope by the power of the Holy Spirit.[29]

As your Father, I care about you, My child, and I want you to be well.

With healing love and grace,

Your heavenly Father

References: *(1) Psalms 103:2-3; (2) 3 John 2; (3) Exodus 23:25; (4) Exodus 15:26; (5) Jeremiah 17:14; (6) Jeremiah 30:17; (7) Philippians 3:19; (8) Isaiah 53:5; (9) 1 Peter 2:24; (10) Hebrews 13:8; (11) Proverbs 4:20; (12) Psalms 107:20; (13) Hebrews 4:12; (14) Proverbs 4:21-22; (15) Proverbs 4:23; (16) Proverbs 17:22; (17) 2 Corinthians 1:20; (18) Ephesians 3:20; (19) Matthew 19:26; (20) Hebrews 6:12; (21) Romans 4:20-21; (22) Jeremiah 1:12; (23) Romans 10:17; (24) Mark 11:22; (25) Mark 11:23; (26) Mark 11:24; (27) Matthew 7:7-8; (28) John 16:23-24; (29) Romans 15:13.*

45

Holiness

Key Thought: You are called to holiness.

Key Scripture: *"Give unto the Lord the glory due to His name; worship the Lord in the beauty of holiness"* (Ps. 29.2, NKJV).

Letter From the Heart of God

My very own child, you will be blessed, as you give Me glory and worship Me in the beauty of holiness.[1] It is My desire, as your heavenly Father, to help you increase and abound in love toward others and to establish your heart blameless in holiness before Me at the coming of your Lord Jesus Christ.[2] Remember, I have not called you to uncleanness, but to holiness.[3]

Therefore, I beseech you, by My mercies to you, to present your body as a living sacrifice, holy, acceptable to Me, for this is your reasonable service of worship. Do not be conformed to this world, but be transformed by the renewing of your mind, that you may prove what My good, acceptable, and perfect will is.[4]

In Christ I chose you as My own, before the foundation of the world, that you should be both holy and blameless before Me in love.[5]

Through the death of My Son, Jesus Christ, I have reconciled you to myself, and His crucifixion enables you to experience holiness, to be blameless, and to be above reproach in My sight. Therefore, I want you to continue in the faith, grounded and steadfast. Never allow yourself to be moved away from the hope of the gospel.[6]

I have chosen you, My child. As one of My holy and beloved children, put on tender mercies, kindness, humility, meekness, and longsuffering. Bear with others and forgive them. Even as Christ forgave you, so you, also, must forgive. Above all these things, put on love, which is the bond of perfection.[7]

Dear one, never forget that it is through My power that you were saved, and through My power I've called you with a holy calling, not according to your own works, but according to My own purpose and grace, which were given to you in Christ Jesus before time began.[8]

Therefore, gird up your mind, be sober, and rest your hope fully upon the grace that is to be brought to you at the revelation of Jesus Christ. As My obedient child, do not allow yourself to be conformed to the former lusts, passions, and desires, as in the ignorance of your former life. Be holy, remembering that I have called you and I am holy. My child, be holy in all your behavior and conduct.[9]

Imitate Me, precious child, and walk in love, as Christ also has loved you and given himself for you.[10] As one who imitates Me, be hospitable, a lover of what is good, sober-minded, just, holy, and self-controlled. Hold fast the faithful word, as you have been taught, so you will be able, by sound doctrine, both to exhort and convict those who contradict it.[11]

I want you to present all your members and faculties as servants of righteousness for holiness and sanctification.[12]

Now that you have been set free from sin, and have become My bondservant, the fruit you reap is holiness and its end, eternal life.[13] As you go about your daily life, keep your mind on the fact that I am your Father and I want you to cleanse yourself from all filthiness of the flesh and spirit, perfecting holiness in reverential fear and awe of Me.[14]

Be continually filled with the Holy Spirit.[15] His fruit in your life is love, joy, peace, patience, kindness, goodness, faithfulness, gentleness, and self-control. Against such there is no law.[16]

You belong to Christ, My child, and you have crucified the flesh with all its passions and desires.[17] Therefore, I want you to live and walk in the Spirit at all times,[18] and you will not fulfill the lusts of the flesh.[19]

In this letter I've stressed the importance of holiness in your life. I do this, My child, because I know that holiness will benefit you in so many ways. I will help you, and I will never leave you nor forsake you.[20] I love you with an everlasting love.[21]

In perfect love and holiness,

God, your Father

References: *(1) Psalms 29:2; (2) 1 Thessalonians 3:12-13; (3) 1 Thessalonians 4:7; (4) Romans 12:1-2; (5) Ephesians 1:4; (6) Colossians 1:22-24; (7) Colossians 3:12-14; (8) 2 Timothy 1:8-9; (9) 1 Peter 1:13-15; (10) Ephesians 5:1-2; (11) Titus 1:8-9; (12) Romans 6:19; (13) Romans 6:22; (14) 2 Corinthians 7:1; (15) Ephesians 5:18; (16) Galatians 5:22-23; (17) Galatians 5:24; (18) Galatians 5:25; (19) Galatians 5:16; (20) Hebrews 13:5; (21) Jeremiah 31:3.*

Now you may wish to write a letter of personal response to God.

46

Hope

Key Thought: Hope is an anchor for your soul.

Key Scripture: *"Blessed be the God and Father of our Lord Jesus Christ, who according to His abundant mercy has begotten us again to a living hope through the resurrection of Jesus Christ from the dead"* (1 Pet. 1:3, NKJV).

Letter From the Heart of God

My dear child, since you have been justified by faith, you now have peace with Me through your Lord Jesus Christ. Through Him you also have access by faith into My grace in which you stand. Therefore, rejoice in the hope of My glory.[1]

Rejoice in the midst of your daily trials, knowing that such trials develop perseverance, and perseverance develops character, and character develops hope.[2] You will not be disappointed by such hope, because My love has been poured into your heart by the Holy Spirit who has been given to you.[3] You will be blessed as you place all your trust in Me,[4] for I am your hope.[5]

Ask Me, and I will give you the spirit of wisdom and revelation in the knowledge of Me, that the eyes of your understanding may be enlightened, so you may know the hope to which I have called you, what are the riches of My glorious inheritance in the saints, and what is the exceeding greatness of My power toward those who believe. This power is in accordance with the working of My infinite might, which I worked in Christ when I raised Him from the dead and made Him to sit at My own right hand in heavenly places.[6]

According to My abundant mercy, you have been born again to a living hope through the Resurrection of Jesus Christ from the dead. That hope is an incorruptible and undefiled inheritance, that can never fade away, being reserved in heaven for you.[7]

Rejoice in this hope, My child.[8] Remember, I am the God of hope, and I fill you with all joy and peace in believing, that you may abound in hope by the power of the Holy Spirit.[9]

See what a great love I have bestowed upon you, that I have called you My child, and such you are. Beloved, now you are My child. It has not yet been revealed what you shall be, but you know that, when Jesus appears, you shall be like Him, for you shall see Him as He is. As you have this hope in you, you purify yourself, even as He is pure.[10]

Be diligent, that you may realize the full assurance of hope until the end. Be an imitator of those who through faith and patience inherit My promises,[11] for faith is the substance of the things you hope for, and faith is the evidence of the things you do not yet see.[12]

I am your hiding place and your shield. Hope in My Word, for I will uphold you according to My Word, that you may live. And, you will never be ashamed for placing your hope in Me.[13]

Continue in the faith, grounded and steadfast, and do not allow yourself to be moved away from the hope of the gospel.[14]

Be hopeful, My child, for I love you with an everlasting love,[15] and remember, Christ within you is the hope of glory.[16]

Grace and hope to you,

Your loving Father

References: *(1) Romans 5:1-2; (2) Romans 5:3-4; (3) Romans 5:5; (4) Jeremiah 17:7; (5) Psalms 71:5; (6) Ephesians 1:17-20; (7) 1 Peter 1:3-4; (8) Romans 12:12; (9) Romans 15:13; (10) 1 John 3:1-3; (11) Hebrews 6:11-12; (12) Hebrews 11:1; (13) Psalms 119:114,116; (14) Colossians 1:23; (15) Jeremiah 31:3; (16) Colossians 1:27.*

Now you may wish to write a letter of personal response to God.

47

Humility

Key Thought: God gives grace to the humble.

Key Scripture: *"Be clothed with humility, for 'God resists the proud, but gives grace to the humble.' Therefore humble yourselves under the mighty hand of God, that He may exalt you in due time, casting all your care upon Him, for He cares for you"* (1 Pet. 5:5-7, NKJV).

Letter From the Heart of God

My dear child, it is very important for you to learn to walk in humility and to avoid being prideful, because I resist the proud, but I give grace to the humble. Therefore, humble yourself under My mighty hand of provision and protection, that I may exalt you in due time. Cast all your cares upon Me, for I can take care of you better than you can take care of yourself.[1]

My power is available to you, and My understanding is infinite.[2] My delight is to lift up the humble.[3] Remember, My child, that I do not delight in the strength of the horse nor in the legs of man. I take pleasure in those who reverence Me, in those who hope in My mercy.[4]

I inhabit eternity. I dwell in the high and holy place and with him who is of a humble and contrite spirit. I revive the spirit of the humble and the heart of the one who is contrite. Your humble and contrite spirit pleases me, for My name is Holy.[5]

Let Jesus be your example. Take His yoke upon you and learn of Him. He is meek and gentle. He is humble and lowly in heart. As you do this, you will find rest for your soul.[6]

Remember what Jesus said in the Beatitudes, "Blessed are the poor in spirit, for theirs is the kingdom of heaven."[7] The poor in spirit are those who are completely trusting in and dependent upon Me. To them belong all the treasures of My kingdom.

By My grace you have been saved from the dominion of the sin of pride,[8] and by My grace I have enabled you to walk in humility. You are not made humble by your own efforts; however, you must make the choice to humble yourself under My mighty hand.[9]

The poor in spirit are those who realize they do not have the personal resources to accomplish this and must depend totally upon Me and My mercy. Humility is an attitude of grace I will work into you by My Holy Spirit, as you choose to be humble and depend on Me.[10]

Trust Me, for I am working within you, both to will and to do of My good pleasure, and humility is My very good pleasure for you.[11]

I have shown you what is good and what My fervent desire is for you, My precious child, which is to do justly, love mercy, and walk humbly with Me.[12]

With much love,

Your mighty God

References: (1) 1 Peter 5:5-7; (2) Psalms 147:5; (3) Psalms 147:6; (4) Psalms 145:10-11; (5) Isaiah 57:15; (6) Matthew 11:29; (7) Matthew 5:3; (8) Romans 6:14; (9) 1 Peter 5:5-7; (10) James 4:6; (11) Philippians 2:13; (12) Micah 6:8.

Now you may wish to write a letter of personal response to God.

48

Inheritance

Key Thought: As God's child, you are His heir – a joint heir with Jesus Christ.

Key Scripture: *"The Spirit Himself bears witness with our spirit that we are the children of God, and if children, then heirs—heirs of God and joint heirs with Christ"* (Rom. 8:16 17, NKJV).

Letter From the Heart of God

Dear one, you are My child, and this makes you My heir and a joint heir with Jesus Christ.[1] You are My heir, and you are a partaker of all My promises in Christ.[2] I spared not My own Son, but delivered Him up for you, that I might, with Him, freely give you all things.[3] Indeed, I have blessed you with every spiritual blessing in the heavenly places in Christ.[4]

In Christ you have obtained an inheritance, being predestined according to My purpose. Remember that I work all things according to the counsel of My will.[5]

I have established My covenant with you, My child.[6] The inheritance I've reserved for you is incorruptible and undefiled. It will never fade away. It is reserved in heaven for you.[7]

I have sealed you with the Holy Spirit of promise. He is the guarantee of your inheritance until the time of the final redemption of the purchased possession, to the praise of My glory.[8] I desire to enlighten the eyes of your understanding, so you will know, not only the hope of My calling and the greatness of My power toward all who believe, but also the riches of the glory of My inheritance in the saints.[9]

My child, walk worthy of Me, fully pleasing Me, being fruitful in every good work and increasing in your knowledge of Me.[10] I will strengthen you with all might, according to My glorious power, for all patience and longsuffering with joy.[11]

Give thanks to Me, for I have qualified you to be a partaker of the inheritance of the saints in light.[12] It gives Me great joy to give this inheritance to you, My child.

Receive My love,

Your everlasting Father

References: *(1) Romans 8:16-17; (2) Ephesians 3:6; (3) Romans 8:32; (4) Ephesians 1:3; (5) Ephesians 1:11; (6) Genesis 17:4; (7) 1 Peter 1:4; (8) Ephesians 1:14; (9) Ephesians 1:18; (10) Colossians 1:10; (11) Colossians 1:11; (12) Colossians 1:12.*

49

Integrity

Key Thought: Let your integrity guide you at all times.

Key Scripture: *"But as for me, I will walk in my integrity"* (Ps. 26:11, NKJV).

Letter From the Heart of God

My precious child, keep walking in your integrity.[1] Let your integrity constantly guide you.[2] Walk as a child of the light.[3] Let not mercy and truth forsake you; bind them about your neck.[4] Remember that, as you walk in your integrity, you will walk uprightly and surely.[5]

You are the salt of the earth.[6] Keep yourself far from any false matters.[7] Serve Me in sincerity, integrity, and truth.[8] Keep your tongue from evil and your lips from speaking guile.[9] When you speak truth, you show forth righteousness and integrity.[10] My child, when you are faithful in that which is least, you shall also be faithful in much.[11]

The path of the just is as the shining light, that shines more and more unto the perfect day.[12] My precious child, do justly, love mercy, and walk humbly with Me.[13]

I call all My children to walk in integrity and I have given you My Spirit to guide you into all truth.[14] He will always lead you to walk in integrity, and, as you are led of My Spirit, you will walk as My child, confident you are on the right path.[15]

With much love,

Your heavenly Father

References: *(1) Psalms 26:11; (2) Proverbs 11:3; (3) Ephesians 5:8; (4) Proverbs 3:3; (5) Proverbs 10:9; (6) Matthew 5:13; (7) Exodus 23:7; (8) Joshua 24:14; (9) Psalms 34:13; (10) Proverbs 12:17; (11) Luke 16:10; (12) Proverbs 4:18; (13) Micah 6:8; (14) John 16:13; (15) Romans 8:14.*

Now you may wish to write a letter of personal response to God.

50

Intercession

Key Thought: When you intercede for others, you bear their burdens with them.

Key Scripture: *"Bear one another's burdens, and so fulfill the law of Christ"* (Gal. 6:2, NKJV).

Letter From the Heart of God

Dearly beloved, bear the burdens of others, for in so doing you will be fulfilling the law of Christ.[1] Lift up your prayers for the remnant that is left and[2] pray for the peace of Jerusalem.[3]

When you pray, I do hear you, My child.[4] Everyone who asks receives.[5] Whatever you ask for in prayer, believing, you shall receive.[6] Watch, therefore, and pray always.[7]

Be anxious for nothing, My child, but in everything by prayer and supplication, with thanksgiving, let your requests be made known to Me, and my peace, which surpasses all understanding, will guard your heart and mind through Christ Jesus.[8]

As you pray for others, remember that the Holy Spirit helps you, by making intercession for you and through you.[9] I am able to search all hearts, and I know what the mind of the Spirit is, because He makes intercession for you and others according to My will.[10] At the

same time, Jesus ever lives to make intercession for the saints, as well.[11]

Therefore, My beloved child, continue to
intercede for others, praying always with all
prayer and supplication in the Spirit, being
watchful to this end with all perseverance and
supplication for all the saints.[12]

Many blessings and much love,

Your loving Father

References: *(1) Galatians 6:2; (2) 2 Kings 19:4; (3)
Psalms 122:6; (4) Psalms 34:17; (5) Matthew 7:7-8; (6)
Matthew 21:22; (7) Luke 21:36; (8) Philippians 4:6-7; (9)
Romans 8:26; (10) Romans 8:27; (11) Hebrews 7:25; (12)
Ephesians 6:18.*

*Now you may wish to write a letter of personal
response to God.*

51

Jesus

Key Thought: Let Jesus be everything to you.

Key Scripture: *"In the beginning was the Word, and the Word was with God, and the Word was God. He was in the beginning with God. All things were made through Him, and without Him nothing was made that was made"* (John 1:1-3, NKJV).

Letter From the Heart of God

Dear one, I want you to know that My Son, Jesus Christ, who is the Living Word, was with Me in the beginning. All things were made through Him, and without Him nothing was made that was made.[1] In Him was life, and the life was the light of men.[2] His light shines in the darkness, and the darkness does not comprehend or overcome it.[3] He is the Word, who became flesh and dwelt among mankind.[4]

I sent Jesus to save you from your sins and to give you eternal life.[5] He is My beloved Son in whom I am well pleased.[6] Always remember that Jesus is indeed the Christ, the Savior of the world.[7] He is the way, the truth, and the life.[8] In Him you will find all the treasures of wisdom and knowledge.[9]

Jesus has been made your wisdom, righteousness, sanctification, and redemption.[10] Though He was rich, yet for your sake He became poor, so that through His poverty you would become rich.[11] He is your peace.[12]

He is before all things, and by Him all things consist.[13] He is the Head of the Body, the Church.[14] My child, you are complete in Him, and He is the Head of all principality and power.[15] He is all and in all.[16]

Let the Word of Christ dwell in you richly.[17] Let Jesus have the preeminence in all things in your life.[18]

Grace and peace to you,

Your heavenly Father

References: (1) John 1:1-3; (2) John 1:4; (3) John 1:5; (4) John 1:14; (5) John 3:16; (6) Matthew 3:17; (7) John 4:42; (8) John 14:6; (9) Colossians 2:3; (10) 1 Corinthians 1:30; (11) 2 Corinthians 8:9; (12) Ephesians 2:14; (13) Colossians 1:17; (14) Colossians 1:18; (15) Colossians 2:10; (16) Colossians 3:11; (17) Colossians 3:16; (18) Colossians 1:18.

Now you may wish to write a letter of personal response to God.

52

Joy

Key Thought: Joy is a form of happiness that is not based on life's circumstances.

Key Scripture: *"Do not sorrow, for the joy of the Lord is your strength"* (Neh. 8:10, NKJV).

Letter From the Heart of God

My dear child, I want you to experience My joy at all times, because My joy will translate as strength in your life.[1] Let your heart rejoice in Me at all times.[2] Place your complete trust in Me, and rejoice. Shout for joy, because I defend you.[3] Be glad in Me, My child.[4] Shout for joy, as you realize that you are upright in heart.[5]

As you seek Me, let your heart rejoice.[6] I desire that you be strengthened with all might, according to My glorious power, unto all patience and endurance with joyfulness.[7] Now that you have made Me your Lord, you know the fullest happiness that is possible.[8]

Find wisdom and gain understanding, and you will experience great joy.[9] This is what I want for you, My child. Therefore, let your heart be merry, for a merry heart will do you good, like a medicine.[10] Rejoice in Me, My child, for I am the God of your salvation.[11]

When you pray to Me in the name of Jesus, you shall receive and your joy will be full.[12] Rejoice in Me.[13] Greatly rejoice, My child, in the realization that the genuineness of your faith, being much more precious than gold that perishes, though it is tested by fire, may be found to praise, honor, and glory at the revelation of Jesus Christ, whom having not seen you love. Though now you do not see Him, yet believing, you rejoice with joy inexpressible and full of glory.[14]

Remember, I rejoice over you with joy; I rest in My love for you, and I rejoice over you with singing.[15]

I joy over you, My child,

Your loving Father

References: *(1) Nehemiah 8:10; (2) 1 Samuel 2:1; (3) Psalms 5:11; (4) Psalms 32:11; (5) Psalms 32:11; (6) Psalms 105:3; (7) Colossians 1:11; (8) Psalms 144:15; (9) Proverbs 3:13; (10) Proverbs 17:22; (11) Habakkuk 3:18; (12) John 16:24; (13) Philippians 3:1; (14) 1 Peter 1:6-8; (15) Zephaniah 3:17.*

Now you may wish to write a letter of personal response to God.

53

Kingdom of God

Key Thought: God's kingdom is within you.

Key Scripture: *"For the kingdom of God is not eating and drinking, but righteousness and peace and joy in the Holy Spirit"* (Rom. 14:17, NKJV).

Letter From the Heart of God

My dear child, I want you to enjoy My kingdom. Remember that it does not consist of eating and drinking, but of righteousness, peace, and joy in the Holy Spirit.[1] Seek first My kingdom and My righteousness, and I promise to add all things unto you.[2] Receive My kingdom as a little child, so you will be able to enter into all I have for you.[3]

You will find My kingdom within you.[4] It is near to you.[5] Do not fear, My child, because I delight in giving you My kingdom.[6] My kingdom consists not in words but in power.[7] Remember the words of Jesus, who said, "No one, having put his hand to the plow, and looking back, is fit" for My kingdom.[8]

You, My child, are a member of My royal family, and this fact makes it possible for you to enjoy My kingdom.[9] The Holy Spirit will empower you[10] and guide you[11] into the fullness of kingdom living.

Therefore, be continually filled afresh with the Holy Spirit[12] and let Him show you the way. Then you will experience the fruit of the Holy Spirit in your life, which is love, joy, peace, longsuffering, kindness, goodness, faithfulness, gentleness, and self-control. Against these there is no law, for these are special attributes that characterize My kingdom.[13]

Receive, enter, and enjoy the rights and privileges of membership in My kingdom, dear child.

Love and blessings,

Your heavenly Father

References: *(1) Romans 14:17; (2) Matthew 6:33; (3) Mark 10:15; (4) Luke 17:21; (5) Luke 10:9; (6) Luke 12:32; (7) 1 Corinthians 4:20; (8) Luke 9:62; (9) Revelation 1:6; (10) Acts 1:8; (11) John 16:13; (12) Ephesians 5:18; (13) Galatians 5:22-23.*

Now you may wish to write a letter of personal response to God.

54

Knowledge

Key Thought: The most important knowledge is knowledge of God.

Key Scripture: *"The Lord is a God of knowledge, and by him actions are weighed"* (1 Sam. 2:3).

Letter From the Heart of God

Dearly beloved, I am a God of knowledge, and by Me actions are weighed.[1] If you keep My precepts, you will understand more than the ancients did.[2] Be wise, My child, and increase in your learning.[3] Your reverential fear of Me is the beginning of all true knowledge.[4]

My dear one, get wisdom, get understanding, and don't ever forget them.[5] Be wise and lay up knowledge for yourself.[6] When you possess spiritual understanding, you will seek knowledge.[7]

Hear and understand My Word.[8] Study to show yourself approved unto Me, a worker who never needs to be ashamed, because you will know how to rightly divide My Word.[9]

My child, may grace and peace be multiplied to you in your knowledge of Me and of Jesus, your Lord.[10] My divine power has given you all things that pertain to life and godliness, through your knowledge of Me.[11]

I have given you My great and precious promises, that through these you will be a partaker of My divine nature, having escaped the corruption that is in the world through lust.[12] Jesus is the Living Word, and in Him you will find all the treasures of wisdom and knowledge.[13]

I encourage you to be diligent to add virtue to your faith and knowledge to your virtue,[14] for this will bring great blessing to your life.

All My love,

Your heavenly Father

References: *(1) 1 Samuel 2:3; (2) Psalms 119:100; (3) Proverbs 1:5; (4) Proverbs 1:7; (5) Proverbs 4:5; (6) Proverbs 10:14; (7) Proverbs 15:14; (8) Matthew 15:10; (9) 2 Timothy 2:15; (10) 2 Peter 1:2; (11) 2 Peter 1:3; (12) 2 Peter 1:4; (13) Colossians 2:2-3; (14) 2 Peter 1:5.*

Now you may wish to write a letter of personal response to God.

55

Knowledge of God

Key Thought: To know God is to know you have a Father who loves you.

Key Scripture: *"Grace and peace be multiplied to you in the knowledge of God and of Jesus our Lord"* (2 Pet. 1:2, NKJV).

Letter From the Heart of God

My dear child, may grace and peace be multiplied to you in the knowledge of Me and of Jesus, your Lord.[1] I want you to know that My divine power has given you all things that pertain to life and godliness, through your knowledge of Me. Never forget that I have called you by glory and virtue.[2]

Always remember that I have given you My exceedingly great and precious promises, that through them you may be a partaker of My divine nature, having escaped the corruption that is in the world through lust.[3]

Know that I am the Lord your God. I have brought you out of bondage.[4] Know Me as your Lord, your God, your Father.[5] Be still, and know that I am your God.[6] Jesus is the way, the truth, and the life, and no one can come to Me, except through Him.[7] No one really knows

Me, unless Jesus reveals Me to them.[8] Be thankful that He has revealed Me to you.

Grow in grace, and in your knowledge of Me.[9]

I love you,

God, your Father

References: *(1) 2 Peter 1:2; (2) 2 Peter 1:3; (3) 2 Peter 1:4; (4) Exodus 29:46; (5) 1 Kings 20:28; (6) Psalms 46:10; (7) John 14:6; (8) Matthew 11:27; (9) 2 Peter 3:18.*

Now you may wish to write a letter of personal response to God.

56

Life

Key Thought: To know God is life; not to know Him is death.

Key Scripture: *"For to be carnally minded is death, but to be spiritually minded is life and peace"* (Rom. 8:6, NKJV).

Letter From the Heart of God

Dearly beloved child, I want you to become spiritually minded, because this will give you life and peace.[1] As you gain spiritual understanding, you will be able to live more fully.[2]

My child, your reverential fear of Me will enable you to prolong your days.[3] In fact, it will be a fountain of life to you.[4] You shall live, and you will know that I am your Lord.[5] Seek Me, and you shall live.[6] Seek good, and not evil, and you shall live.[7]

In Jesus you find life, and you discover that His life is the light of all mankind.[8] Indeed, He is the way, the truth, and the life for you, and you cannot come to Me unless you do so through Him.[9] My Son, Jesus, has come to give you life, a more abundant life than you can possibly imagine.[10]

Remember that, if the same Spirit that raised Christ Jesus from the dead dwells in you, He shall quicken your mortal body. Indeed, He will give you life and strength.[11]

The law of the Spirit of life in Christ Jesus had made you free from the law of sin and death.[12] The Spirit gives you life, but the flesh avails nothing. The words that I speak to you are spirit and they are life.[13]

Because Jesus lives, you shall live also.[14] In Him you live, and move, and have your being.[15] When you have My Son, you have life,[16] and the life that you now live in the flesh, you live by faith in My Son, who loved you and gave himself for you.[17] Live for Me, My dear child.

Love and grace to you,

God, your living Father

References: *(1) Romans 8:6; (2) Psalms 119:144; (3) Proverbs 10:27; (4) Proverbs 14:27; (5) Ezekiel 37:6; (6) Amos 5:6; (7) Amos 5:14; (8) John 1:4; (9) John 14:6; (10) John 10:10; (11) Romans 8:11; (12) Romans 8:2; (13) John 6:63; (14) John 14:19; (15) Acts 17:28; (16) 1 John 5:12; (17) Galatians 2:20.*

Now you may wish to write a letter of personal response to God.

57

Light

Key Thought: It takes only a small light to dispel the darkness.

Key Scripture: *"Ye are the light of the world. A city that is set on an hill cannot be hid"* (Matt. 5:14).

Letter From the Heart of God

Dear child, you are the light of the world.[1] Take heed, therefore, that the light which is in you contains no darkness at all.[2] I am your light and your salvation. Therefore, whom shall you fear? I am the strength of your life. Therefore, of whom shall you be afraid?[3]

Let your light so shine before others, that they may see your good works and glorify Me.[4] In Jesus you find life, and His life is your light.[5] Indeed, He is the Light of the world.[6] His light shines in the darkness, but the darkness does not comprehend or overcome it.[7]

You, however, have become light; therefore, be sure to walk as a child of the light, for the fruit of the Spirit is in all goodness, righteousness, and truth, finding out what is acceptable to Me. Have no fellowship with the unfruitful works of darkness, but rather expose them.[8]

My child, you are of a chosen generation, a royal priesthood, a holy nation. You are one of My very special people. Your job is to proclaim My praises, for I have called you out of darkness into My marvelous light.[9] Always remember, My dear child, that I am light, and in Me there is no darkness at all.[10]

Keep on walking in the light as I am in the light, and this will enable you to enjoy true fellowship with both Me and others, and the blood of Jesus Christ, My Son, will cleanse you from all sin.[11]

With much love,

Your heavenly Father

References: *(1) Matthew 5:14; (2) Luke 11:35; (3) Psalms 27:1; (4) Matthew 5:16; (5) John 1:4; (6) John 9:5; (7) John 1:5; (8) Ephesians 5:8-11; (9) 1 Peter 2:9; (10) 1 John 1:5; (11) 1 John 1:3-7.*

Now you may wish to write a letter of personal response to God.

58

Lordship of Christ

Key Thought: Jesus is either Lord of all in your life, or He is not Lord in your life at all.

Key Scripture: *"Therefore God also has highly exalted Him and given Him the name which is above every name, that at the name of Jesus every knee should bow, of those in heaven, and of those on earth, and of those under the earth, and that every tongue should confess that Jesus Christ is Lord, to the glory of God the Father"* (Phil. 2:9-11, NKJV).

Letter From the Heart of God

My dearly beloved child, I have highly exalted Jesus by giving Him the name which is above every name. It is My ultimate plan and purpose that at the name of Jesus every knee shall bow, in heaven and on earth and under the earth, and every tongue confess that Jesus Christ is Lord, to My glory.[1]

Be sure to make Jesus the Lord of every area of your life, for He is before all things and by Him all things consist.[2] His Lordship is the fount of abundant life for you.[3] My child, you are complete in Him, for He is the Head of all principality and power.[4] He is the King of kings and Lord of lords,[5] and He shall reign over all creation forever and ever.[6] My Son, Jesus Christ, is all, and He is in all.[7]

Therefore, let the Word of Christ dwell in you richly.[8] Be strong in the grace that you find in Christ Jesus.[9] Jesus is the Author and Finisher of your faith.[10] Give glory to Him both now and forever.[11]

Always know that Jesus, who lives within you, is far greater than he who is in the world.[12] I sent Him into the world so you would be able to live through Him.[13] For all of these reasons, My child, I implore you to make Jesus the absolute Lord of your life.

Grace and peace to you,

Your heavenly Father

References: *(1) Philippians 2:2; (2) Colossians 1:17; (3) John 10:10; (4) Colossians 2:10; (5) 1 Timothy 6:15; (6) Isaiah 9:7; (7) Colossians 3:11; (8) Colossians 3:16; (9) 2 Timothy 2:1; (10) Hebrews 12:2; (11) 2 Peter 3:18; (12) 1 John 4:4; (13) 1 John 4:9.*

Now you may wish to write a letter of personal response to God.

59

Love

Key Thought: If love is your motive, you cannot go wrong.

Key Scripture: *"And now abide faith, hope, love, these three; but the greatest of these is love"* (1 Cor. 13:13, NKJV).

Letter From the Heart of God

My child, I love you. Remember that faith, hope, and love abide, but the greatest of these is love.[1] Therefore, pursue love, and desire spiritual gifts.[2] By this shall all people know that you are a disciple of Christ, that you have love for others.[3] Let your love be without hypocrisy at all times.[4]

Owe no one anything except to love him.[5] When you practice love, you fulfill My law.[6] Remember that love works no ill to your neighbor.[7] Let everything you do be done with love.[8]

By love serve others.[9] All the law is fulfilled in one word, even in this: you shall love your neighbor as yourself.[10] In Christ that which avails is faith working through love.[11]

My child, walk in love, as Christ has loved you.[12] Above everything else put on love, which is the bond of perfection.[13] Don't just love in word or speech, but love in deed and in truth.[14]

Remember that, when you dwell in love, you are actually dwelling in Me and I am dwelling in you.[15] My perfect love casts out all fear.[16] Love Me, My child, remembering that I have first loved you.[17]

All My love,

Your Abba Father

References: *(1) 1 Corinthians 13:13; (2) 1 Corinthians 14:1; (3) John 13:35; (4) Romans 12:9; (5) Romans 13:8; (6) Romans 13:10; (7) Romans 13:10; (8) 1 Corinthians 16:14; (9) Galatians 5:13; (10) Galatians 5:14; (11) Galatians 5:6; (12) Ephesians 5:2; (13) Colossians 3:14; (14) 1 John 3:18; (15) 1 John 4:16; (16) 1 John 4:18; (17) 1 John 4:19.*

Now you may wish to write a letter of personal response to God.

60

Loving God

Key Thought: Love God with all your heart.

Key Scripture: *"Love the Lord thy God"* (Deut. 19:9).

Letter From the Heart of God

Dearly beloved, simply love Me.[1] I want so much for you to learn to love Me with all your heart, with all your soul, and with all your might.[2] Take good heed to the importance of loving Me.[3] As you learn to love Me more fully, you will become radiant and will shine like the sun.[4]

Set your love upon me, and I will deliver you and set you on high. Call upon me, and I will answer you. I will be with you in times of trouble and will deliver you and honor you. I will satisfy you with long life and show you My salvation.[5]

As the deer pants after the mountain brooks, let your soul pant after Me.[6] The first and greatest commandment is that you should love Me with all your heart, with all your soul, and with all your mind.[7] This is the supreme commandment that you must follow, My child, because all things work together for good in the life of one who truly loves Me.[8]

Your eye has not seen and your ear has not heard all the things I have prepared for you, because you love Me.[9]

Keep yourself in My love and keep on looking for the mercy of your Lord Jesus Christ.[10] Love others, as well, because love is born of Me. Indeed, I am love.[11] I manifested My love to the world by sending My only begotten Son, so that you would be able to live through Him eternally.[12]

Remember that you are able to love Me, because I first lavished My love upon you.[13] Love Me, My child, for I love you with an everlasting love and with lovingkindness I have drawn you to myself.[14]

With love and blessing,

Your Abba Father

References: *(1) Deuteronomy 10:12; (2) Deuteronomy 6:5; (3) Joshua 23:11; (4) Judges 5:31; (5) Psalms 91:14-16; (6) Psalms 42:1; (7) Matthew 22:37-38; (8) Romans 8:28; (9) 1 Corinthians 2:9; (10) Jude 21; (11) 1 John 4:7-8; (12) 1 John 4:9; (13) 1 John 4:19; (14) Jeremiah 31:3.*

Now you may wish to write a letter of personal response to God.

61

Materialism

Key Thought: What you see will pass away; what you don't see is eternal.

Key Scripture: *"Do not lay up for yourselves treasures on earth, where moth and rust destroy and where thieves break in and steal; but lay up for yourselves treasures in heaven, where neither moth nor rust destroys and where thieves do not break in and steal. For where your treasure is, there your heart will be also"* (Matt. 6:19-21, NKJV).

Letter From the Heart of God

My precious child, keep eternal values and verities in focus as you go about your daily life. Do not lay up treasures on earth, but lay up treasures in heaven, for where your treasure is, there your heart will be also.[1] Treasure stored up with Me keeps your heart close to Me.

Always remember that you do not live by bread only, but by every word that proceeds from My mouth.[2] You cannot serve both materialism and Me.[3] Therefore, I want you to seek first My kingdom and My righteousness, and, as you do that, I promise to take care of your every need.[4]

What profit would it be for you to gain the whole world and still lose your own soul?[5]

Your life does not consist in the abundance of the things you own.[6] Therefore, labor for those things which endure unto everlasting life.[7]

My child, always remember that My kingdom does not consist of meat and drink, but righteousness, peace, and joy in the Holy Spirit.[8] These are the things I want for you, My child.

I want you to remember always that the things you see are temporal and last only a short while, but the things which are unseen go on forever.[9] Therefore, do not allow the cares of this world and the deceitfulness of riches to choke the Word and render your life unproductive of eternal spiritual fruit.[10]

I beseech you to set your affections on things above, not on things that are on the earth.[11] Love not the world, neither the things that are in the world.[12] Rather, love that which makes you eternally wealthy!

All My love to you,

Your heavenly Father

References: (1) Matthew 6:19-21; (2) Deuteronomy 8:3; (3) Matthew 6:24; (4) Matthew 6:33; (5) Mark 8:36; (6) Luke 12:15; (7) John 6:27; (8) Romans 14:17; (9) 2 Corinthians 4:18; (10) Matthew 13:22-23; (11) Colossians 3:2; (12) 1 John 2:15.

62

Meekness

Key Thought: Meekness is not weakness; it is strength under control.

Key Scripture: *"The meek shall eat and be satisfied: they shall praise the Lord that seek him"* (Ps. 22:26).

Letter From the Heart of God

My dear child, as you practice meekness in your life, you will experience satisfaction.[1] As a result of your meekness, I will guide you in judgment and teach you My ways.[2] You must always remember that the meek shall inherit the earth.[3]

If you will walk in meekness, I will lift you up.[4] Therefore, take Jesus' yoke upon you and learn from Him to be meek and lowly in heart. Then, you shall find rest for your soul.[5]

My child, be continually filled with the Holy Spirit.[6] The fruit of the Spirit in your life will include meekness, along with love, joy, peace, patience, kindness, goodness, faithfulness, and self-control.[7] Walking in meekness will bring great joy, happiness, blessedness, and spiritual prosperity to you.[8]

Remember that I am always near to those who have a broken heart and a contrite spirit;

near to all those who are meek.[9] Walk humbly
with Me, My child.[10] Be clothed with meekness
and humility.[11] All of your sufficiency comes
from Me.[12]

With much love,

Your faithful Father

References: *(1) Psalms 22:26; (2) Psalms 25:9; (3) Psalms
37:11; (4) Psalms 147:6; (5) Matthew 11:29; (6) Ephesians
5:18; (7) Galatians 5:22-23; (8) Matthew 5:5; (9) Psalms
34:18; (10) Micah 6:8; (11) 1 Peter 5:5; (12) 2 Corinthians
3:5.*

*Now you may wish to write a letter of personal
response to God.*

63

Mercy of God

Key Thought: God is merciful.

Key Scripture: *"The Lord thy God is a merciful God"* (Deut. 4:31).

Letter From the Heart of God

My dear child, always know that I am full of mercy.[1] I beseech you, by My mercies to you, that you would present your body as a living sacrifice, holy, acceptable to Me, because this is your reasonable service of worship.[2]

Do not be conformed to this world, but be transformed by the renewing of your mind, that you may prove what is My good, acceptable, and perfect will.[3]

I am merciful, and I do not hold onto anger.[4] In fact, mercies and forgiveness belong to Me.[5] Therefore, I ask you to be merciful in the same way that I am merciful.[6] When you practice mercy, you shall receive My mercy and experience great joy, happiness, blessedness, and spiritual prosperity.[7]

What do I require of you, My child? I require that you do justly, love mercy, and walk humbly with Me.[8] Give thanks to Me, remembering that My mercy truly endures forever.[9]

I am the Father of mercies and the God of all comfort, and I desire to comfort you in all your troubles.[10] Therefore, My child, come boldly to My throne of grace to obtain My mercy and find My grace to help you in your time of need.[11]

By My abundant mercy you have been born again to a living hope through the Resurrection of Jesus Christ from the dead, to an inheritance, incorruptible, undefiled, that will not fade away, reserved for you in heaven.[12]

Never forget that I am rich in mercy, and I have great love for you.[13]

Many blessings, My child,

Your merciful Father

References: *(1) Deuteronomy 4:31; (2) Romans 12:1; (3) Romans 12:2; (4) Jeremiah 3:12; (5) Daniel 9:9; (6) Luke 6:36; (7) Matthew 5:7; (8) Micah 6:8; (9) 1 Chronicles 16:34; (10) 2 Corinthians 1:3-4; (11) Hebrews 4:16; (12) 1 Peter 1:3-4; (13) Ephesians 2:4.*

Now you may wish to write a letter of personal response to God.

64

Ministry

Key Thought: Each person you meet is an opportunity to minister.

Key Scripture: *"Freely you have received, freely give"* (Matt. 10:8, NKJV).

Letter From the Heart of God

Dearly beloved, remember all that you have freely received from Me, and this will propel you to give freely wherever you go.[1] Keep on serving Me in sincerity and in truth.[2] Feed My lambs,[3] and feed My sheep.[4]

The harvest truly is plentiful, but the laborers are few. Therefore, you are needed, and pray that others will join in the ministry as well.[5]

Serve Me with humility, My child.[6] Remember that, as you minister, you labor together with Me.[7] Be steadfast, unmovable, always abounding in My work, forasmuch as you know that your labor is not in vain.[8]

To every believer I have entrusted the ministry of reconciliation,[9] so do not think you have no ministry. You are an ambassador for Christ wherever you go, beseeching the lost to be reconciled to Me.[10]

As you have opportunity, always do good unto other people.[11] Bear the burdens of others, for in doing so you are actually fulfilling the law of Christ.[12] If you see someone overtaken in any sin, restore such a one in a spirit of gentleness, considering yourself lest you also be tempted.[13]

Preach the Word! Be ready in season and out of season. Convince, rebuke, exhort, with all longsuffering and teaching.[14] Sanctify Christ in your heart and always be ready to give an answer to everyone who asks of you a reason for the hope that is within you, doing it with meekness and reverence.[15]

Be diligent to present yourself as one approved of Me, a worker who never needs to be ashamed, having rightly divided My Word.[16] Walk closely with Me and depend upon Me, for I want you to speak My words as you minister and to serve in the strength I supply.[17]

Know, My child, that you are able to minister, because you are My workmanship, created in Christ Jesus unto good works.[18]

With love and grace,

God, your Father

References: (1) Matthew 10:8; (2) Joshua 24:14; (3) John 21:15; (4) John 21:16-17; (5) Matthew 9:37-38; (6) Acts 20:19; (7) 1 Corinthians 3:9; (8) 1 Corinthians 15:58; (9) 2 Corinthians 5:18; (10) 2 Corinthians 5:20; (11) Galatians 6:10; (12) Galatians 6:2; (13) Galatians 6:1; (14) 2 Timothy 4:2; (15) 1 Peter 3:15; (16) 2 Timothy 2:15; (17) 1 Peter 4:11; (18) Ephesians 2:10.

65

Needs

Key Thought: Your greatest need is God, and His greatness will meet your every need.

Key Scripture: *"And my God shall supply all your need according to His riches in glory by Christ Jesus"* (Phil. 4:19, NKJV).

Letter From the Heart of God

My dear child, look to Me to supply all of your needs according to My riches in glory by Christ Jesus.[1] Seek first My kingdom and My righteousness, and I promise to take care of your needs.[2]

Always remember that I know what things you need, even before you express them to Me.[3] Therefore, do not cast away your confidence, for it has great reward.[4] Be an imitator of those who, through faith and patience, inherit the promises.[5]

Come boldly to the throne of My grace that you may obtain My mercy and find My grace to help in your time of need.[6] Pursue righteousness, godliness, faith, love, patience, and gentleness. Fight the good fight of faith and take hold of eternal life to which you were called.[7]

Have faith in Me.[8] And, whatever things you ask for in prayer, believe that you receive them, and you shall have them.[9]

Trust in Me, and do good.[10] Delight yourself in Me, and I will give you the desires of your heart.[11] Commit your way to Me as you trust in Me, and I will bring it to pass.[12]

My child, always remember that My grace is sufficient for you.[13] I always give more grace to those who humble themselves before Me.[14] Therefore, submit yourself to Me. Resist the devil, and he will flee from you.[15]

Draw near to Me, and I will draw near to you.[16] Humble yourself in My sight, and I will lift you up.[17] Because I love you, I want to meet your every need.

With much love,

Your all-sufficient Father

References: *(1) Philippians 4:19; (2) Matthew 6:33; (3) Matthew 6:8; (4) Hebrews 10:35; (5) Hebrews 6:12; (6) Hebrews 4:16; (7) 1 Timothy 6:11-12; (8) Mark 11:22; (9) Mark 11:24; (10) Psalms 37:3; (11) Psalms 37:4; (12) Psalms 37:5; (13) 2 Corinthians 12:9; (14) James 4:6; (15) James 4:7; (16) James 4:8; (17) James 4:10.*

Now you may wish to write a letter of personal response to God.

66

New Life in Christ

Key Thought: Life in Christ is the most exciting life of all.

Key Scripture: *"Therefore, if anyone is in Christ, He is a new creation; old things have passed away; behold, all things have become new"* (2 Cor. 5:17, NKJV).

Letter From the Heart of God

Dearly beloved, I am writing to remind you of who you are in Christ and the blessings you have in Him. First, because you are in Christ, you are a completely new creation. The old things have passed away, and all things have become new.[1] You have been born again, not of perishable seed, but imperishable, through My ever-living and abiding Word.[2]

I have delivered you from the power of darkness and brought you into the Kingdom of the Son of My love. In Him you have redemption through His blood and the forgiveness of your sins.[3] Let your heart be encouraged, My child, and knit together in love with other believers, so that you may have all the riches of the full assurance of understanding and the knowledge of My mystery, of Christ, in whom are hid all the treasures of wisdom and knowledge.[4]

As you have received Christ Jesus as your Lord, so walk in Him, rooted and built up in Him and established in the faith, as you have been taught, abounding therein with thanksgiving.[5] My child, you are complete in Christ, who is the Head of all principality and power.[6]

You have been raised with Christ; therefore, seek those things which are above, where He is sitting at My right hand. Set your mind on things above, not on things on the earth, for you have died and your life is hidden with Christ in Me.[7]

I have blessed you with every spiritual blessing in the heavenly realms in Christ.[8] In Him you have obtained an inheritance, being predestined according to My purpose[9] to be a joint-heir with Jesus Christ, your Lord.[10] My child, in Christ you were sealed with the Holy Spirit of promise, who has been given as the guarantee of your inheritance.[11]

In My rich mercy and great love for you I have made you alive with Christ, have raised you up with Him, and seated you with Him in the heavenly places in Christ Jesus.[12] You are My workmanship, created in Christ Jesus unto good works, which I prepared beforehand that you should walk in them.[13]

You are not a stranger or foreigner, but a fellow-citizen with all saints, and a member of My household.[14] Therefore, be renewed in the spirit of your mind and put on the new self, created after My likeness in true righteousness and holiness.[15]

Be a follower of Me, as My dear child, and walk in love, just as Christ loved you and gave himself up for you, a fragrant offering and sacrifice to Me.[16] Be continually filled with the Holy Spirit[17] and be strong in Me and in the power of My might.[18]

Give no place to the devil.[19] I resist the proud and give grace to the humble. Therefore, submit yourself to Me. Resist the devil, and he will flee from you. Draw near to Me, and I will draw near to you.[20] Humble yourself in My sight, and I will lift you up.[21]

If I am for you, who can be successful against you?[22] No weapon that is formed against you will prosper, and every tongue that rises against you in judgment you shall condemn. For this is the heritage of My servants, whose righteousness is of Me.[23]

In all things you are more than a conqueror through Christ who loves you.[24] You can do all things through the strength He imparts to you.[25] My child, nothing can ever

separate you from My love, which is in Christ
Jesus, your Lord.[26]

I love you, My child,

Your faithful Father

References: *(1) 2 Corinthians 5:17; (2) 1 Peter 1:23; (3)
Colossians 1:13-14; (4) Colossians 2:2-3; (5) Colossians
2:6-7; (6) Colossians 2:10; (7) Colossians 3:1-3; (8)
Ephesians 1:3; (9) Ephesians 1:11; (10) Romans 8:17; (11)
Ephesians 1:13; (12) Ephesians 2:4-6; (13) Ephesians 2:10;
(14) Ephesians 2:19; (15) Ephesians 4:23-24; (16)
Ephesians 5:1-2; (17) Ephesians 5:18; (18) Ephesians 6:10;
(19) Ephesians 4:27; (20) James 4:6-8; (21) James 4:10;
(22) Romans 8:31; (23) Isaiah 54:17; (24) Romans 8:37;
(25) Philippians 4:13; (26) Romans 8:39.*

*Now you may wish to write a letter of personal
response to God.*

67

Obedience

Key Thought: Obeying God brings spiritual freedom.

Key Scripture: *"By this we know that we love the children of God, when we love God and keep His commandments. And His commandments are not burdensome. For whatever is born of God overcomes the world. And this is the victory that has overcome the world—our faith"* (1 John 5:2-4, NKJV).

Letter From the Heart of God

My precious child, I'm writing this letter, so you will know how important your obedience is to Me. As your loving Father, I want you to keep My commandments. They are for your good and are not burdensome in any respect. Never forget that you are My child, born of Me, and this enables you to be an overcomer. In fact, your faith is the victory that overcomes the world.[1]

My child, always love in deed and in truth. Knowing you are of the truth will reassure your heart before Me, whenever your heart condemns you. Always remember that I am greater than your heart, and I know all things. Beloved, if your heart does not condemn you, you have confidence before Me and you receive whatever you ask from Me, because you keep My commandments and do what is pleasing in My sight.[2]

This is My commandment to you: Believe on the name of My Son, Jesus Christ, and love others. In so doing, you will abide in Me, and I will abide in you. You will know that I live and abide within you by the Spirit I've given to you.[3]

My grace is at work in your life to enable you to obey Me, and it is always sufficient for you. In fact, My grace is made perfect in your weaknesses.[4] Sin shall not have dominion over you, for you are not under law but under grace.[5] Therefore, present yourself as a true servant of obedience that leads to righteousness.[6]

Though you walk in the flesh, My child, you do not conduct spiritual warfare according to the flesh. The weapons of your warfare are not carnal, but they are mighty through My power for pulling down strongholds, casting down reasonings and every high thing that exalts itself against the knowledge of Me. Therefore, take all your thoughts captive to the obedience of Christ.[7]

As My obedient child, be strong in Me and in the power of My might. Put on all the armor I've provided for you, that you may be able to stand against the wiles of the devil.[8]

When you ask yourself, "What does the Father require of me?" remember that I've shown you what is good and what I require of you. I want you to do justly, to love mercy, and to walk humbly with Me.[9]

Be continually filled with the Spirit,[10] and never forget that I am able to do exceeding abundantly beyond all you can ask or think, according to My power that is at work within you.[11] Look to Me, My child, for I am the God of peace who is able to sanctify you completely. I have called you, and I will be faithful to help you do what I've called you to do.[12]

Walk in the light as I am in the light. In this way you will have fellowship with Me, Jesus, and your fellow-believers,[13] and the blood of Jesus Christ will cleanse you from all sin.[14] Be sure to walk in the light, My child, and remember that My Word is a lamp unto your feet and a light unto your path.[15]

If you confess your sins, I will be faithful and just to forgive you of your sins and to cleanse you from all unrighteousness.[16] You are My precious child. Walk in My ways, that it may go well with you.[17]

I manifested My love for you by sending My Son, Jesus Christ, into the world, that you might live through Him. In this is love, that I sent My Son to be the sacrifice for your sins.[18] Because I love you so much, My child, I want you to enjoy the blessings of obedience at all times.

With all My love,

Your heavenly Father

References: (1) 1 John 5:2-4; (2) 1 John 3:18-22; (3) 1 John 3:23-24; (4) 2 Corinthians 12:9; (5) Romans 6:14; (6) Romans 6:16; (7) 2 Corinthians 10:3-5; (8) Ephesians 6:10-11; (9) Micah 6:8; (10) Ephesians 5:18; (11) Ephesians 3:20; (12) 1 Thessalonians 5:23-24; (13) 1 John 1:3; (14) 1 John 1:7; (15) Psalms 119:105; (16) 1 John 1:9; (17) Jeremiah 7:23; (18) 1 John 4:9-10.

Now you may wish to write a letter of personal response to God.

68

Patience

Key Thought: Patience is a primary virtue.

Key Scripture: *"And we desire that each one of you show the same diligence to the full assurance of hope until the end, that you do not become sluggish, but imitate those who through faith and patience inherit the promises"* (Heb. 6:11-12, NKJV).

Letter From the Heart of God

My dear child, it is through faith and enduring patience that you inherit My promises.[1] Therefore, I ask you to wait on Me and be of good courage, and let your heart be strong and patient.[2] Wait on Me and you will never be ashamed, for I will show you My ways, teach you My paths, and lead you in My truth.[3]

Remember, I am your help and your shield.[4] Though My promise or an answer to your prayers seems to tarry, keep on waiting for it, for it will surely come.[5] Wait for My promise to be fulfilled.[6] All of My promises are yes and amen in Christ Jesus, your Lord.[7]

As you wait upon Me, you will find both your spiritual and physical strength renewed.[8] Like a farmer who waits for the harvest and has long patience for it, you be patient, also, and establish your heart in the certainty of My promises.[9]

Stay joyful and don't be concerned, if the answer takes awhile, knowing that the trying of your faith works patience. When patience has had her perfect work, you will be mature and whole, lacking nothing.[10]

My child, do not grow weary in well doing, for in due season you will reap, if you do not lose heart.[11] Be gentle to everyone, apt to teach, and patient.[12] Be swift to hear, slow to speak, and slow to anger.[13]

When you do well and still suffer for it, but bear it patiently, this is acceptable and well-pleasing to Me.[14] Be continually filled with the Holy Spirit, My child,[15] for He will work within you to produce His fruit of patience in your life.[16]

Patience will be such a blessing to you, My child.

Rest in Me,

Your loving Father

References: *(1) Hebrews 10:36; (2) Psalms 27:14; (3) Psalms 25:3-5; (4) Psalms 33:20; (5) Habakkuk 2:3; (6) Acts 1:4; (7) 2 Corinthians 1:20; (8) Isaiah 40:21; (9) James 5:7-8; (10) James 1:2-4; (11) Galatians 6:9; (12) 2 Timothy 2:24; (13) James 1:19; (14) 1 Peter 2:20; (15) Ephesians 5:18; (16) Galatians 5:22-23.*

69

Peace

Key Thought: The peace God gives to you surpasses all understanding.

Key Scripture: *"And let the peace of God rule in your hearts, to which also you were called in one body; and be thankful"* (Col. 3:15, NKJV).

Letter From the Heart of God

My beloved child, let My peace rule in your heart, and be thankful.[1] Seek peace, and pursue it.[2] When your ways are pleasing to Me, I will make even your enemies to be at peace with you.[3] Therefore, love My truth and My peace.[4]

Jesus has given you His peace. This peace is not the absence of war, strife, confusion, chaos, and pressure, which the world calls peace; but, it is a peace you can hold onto, even in the midst of those things. For it is not outer peace but inner peace that Jesus has given you. Therefore, don't let your heart be troubled and don't let it be afraid.[5]

You have peace with Me through Jesus Christ.[6] In fact, He is your peace.[7] Always remember that I am never the author of confusion, but always of peace.[8] Therefore, I want you to let My peace rule in your heart.[9]

Always be at peace with your fellow-believers.[10] Be anxious for nothing, but in everything by prayer and supplication, with thanksgiving, let your requests be made known unto Me, and My peace, which surpasses all understanding will guard your heart and mind through Christ Jesus.[11]

My child, turn away from all evil and do good; seek peace and pursue it.[12] Never forget that I will keep you in perfect peace, as you keep your mind stayed on Me, because you steadfastly trust in Me. Trust in Me forever, for I am your everlasting Rock.[13]

In perfect peace,

Your heavenly Father

References: *(1) Colossians 3:15; (2) Psalms 34:14; (3) Proverbs 16:7; (4) Zechariah 8:19; (5) John 14:27; (6) Romans 5:1; (7) Ephesians 2:14; (8) 1 Corinthians 14:33; (9) Colossians 3:15; (10) 1 Thessalonians 5:13; (11) Philippians 4:6-7; (12) 1 Peter 3:10-11; (13) Isaiah 26:3-4.*

Now you may wish to write a letter of personal response to God.

70

Persecution

Key Thought: Christ has overcome all persecution and evil.

Key Scripture: *"Blessed are they which are persecuted for righteousness' sake: for theirs is the kingdom of heaven"* (Matt. 5:10).

Letter From the Heart of God

My dearly loved child, even if you are persecuted for righteousness' sake, remember that yours is the kingdom of heaven.[1] Blessed are you, when others shall revile you and persecute you and shall say all manner of evil against you falsely for My sake. Rejoice and be exceedingly glad, for your reward in heaven is great.[2]

Pray for all those who despitefully use you and persecute you.[3] Do not be surprised if others will hate you for My name's sake, but always remember that you shall be rewarded, if you endure until the end.[4]

Don't fear those which are able to kill your body, but are not able to kill your soul.[5] When others despise and reject you for being a Christian, they are also despising and rejecting Me.[6] If the world hates you, remember that it hated Me before it hated you.[7] Because they have persecuted Jesus, you can be sure that they will persecute you, as well.[8]

Bless those who persecute you. Bless them, don't curse them.[9] Endure hardness as a good soldier of Jesus Christ.[10] All who are determined to live a godly life in Christ Jesus will suffer persecution.[11]

However, if you are persecuted as a Christian, do not be ashamed but give praise to Me that you are privileged to bear that name.[12] Do not fear persecution, My child,[13] for My perfect love for you casts out all fear.[14]

Be strong in Me,

Your faithful Father

References: *(1) Matthew 5:10; (2) Matthew 5:11-12; (3) Matthew 5:44; (4) Matthew 10:22; (5) Matthew 10:28; (6) Luke 10:16; (7) John 15:18; (8) John 15:20; (9) Romans 12:14; (10) 2 Timothy 2:3; (11) 2 Timothy 3:12; (12) 1 Peter 4:16; (13) Revelation 2:10; (14) 1 John 4:18.*

Now you may wish to write a letter of personal response to God.

71

Perseverance

Key Thought: Perseverance does not give up in the face of any obstacle, opposition, or discouragement.

Key Scripture: *"Therefore, among God's churches we boast about your perseverance and faith in all the persecutions and trials you are enduring"* (2 Thess. 1:4, NIV).

Letter From the Heart of God

My dear child, hold fast the confession of your hope without wavering, because I promise to be faithful to you at all times.[1] I will strengthen your hands.[2] Who shall separate you from the love of Christ? Shall tribulation, or distress, or persecution, or famine, or nakedness, or peril, or sword?[3] No, in all these things you are more than a conqueror through Christ.[4]

Persevere, My child, and be fully persuaded that neither death nor life, nor angels nor principalities nor powers, nor things present nor things to come, nor height nor depth, nor any other created thing, shall ever be able to separate you from My love, which you find in Jesus Christ, your Lord.[5]

Be watchful and persevere in prayer at all times in the Spirit with all kinds of prayer and supplication for all the saints.[6] My child, lay aside every weight, and the sin which so easily ensnares you, and run with endurance the race that is set before you.[7]

Keep on looking to Jesus, who is the Author and Finisher of your faith, who, for the joy that was set before Him, endured the cross, despising the shame, and is now seated at My right hand.[8]

Remember, My child, that tribulation produces perseverance in your life.[9] Perseverance, likewise, will produce character in your life, and character will produce hope.[10] Never forget that hope does not disappoint, because My love has been poured out in your heart by the Holy Spirit, whom I have given to you.[11]

Be encouraged, My child, for here with Me is a great cloud of witnesses, who have persevered before you, and they join Me in cheering you on.[12]

Lovingly,

Your unchanging Father

References: *(1) Hebrews 10:23; (2) Nehemiah 6:9; (3) Romans 8:35; (4) Romans 8:37; (5) Romans 8:38-39; (6) Ephesians 6:18; (7) Hebrews 12:1; (8) Hebrews 12:2; (9) Romans 5:3; (10) Romans 5:4; (11) Romans 5:5; (12) Hebrews 12:1.*

72

Power

Key Thought: Dynamic power is available to you through the Holy Spirit.

Key Scripture: *"God has spoken once, twice I have heard this: that power belongs to God"* (Ps. 62:11, NKJV).

Letter From the Heart of God

My dear child, always remember that power truly does belong to Me.[1] When I open a door, no one can shut it; and when I close a door, no one can open it.[2] My kingdom is not in word, but it is in power.[3]

I want you to know that you can accomplish great things through Me, My child, but it is not done by your might nor by your power, but by My Spirit.[4] In fact, I impart My power to you through the Holy Spirit, enabling you to be a witness for Me wherever you go.[5]

Do not ever be ashamed of the Gospel of Jesus Christ, for it is My power unto salvation to all who believe.[6] It is My desire to give you the spirit of wisdom and revelation, that you may know Me better[7] and to enlighten the eyes of your understanding. Then you will know the hope of My calling, the riches of the glory of My inheritance in the saints,[8] and the exceeding greatness of My power toward all who believe.[9]

It is this same power which was at work in Christ, when I raised Him from the dead and seated Him at My right hand in the heavenly places,[10] far above all principality and power and might and dominion and every name that is named, not only in this age, but also in that which is to come.[11]

I am able to do exceedingly abundantly above all that you can ask or think, through My power which is at work in you and through you.[12] Know that, in Christ, I will always lead you in triumph, and, through you, I will spread the fragrance of the knowledge of Me everywhere.[13]

My child, be continually filled with My Spirit[14] and be strong in Me and in the power of My might.[15]

Abundant blessings to you,

Your mighty Father

References: (1) Psalms 62:11; (2) Isaiah 22:22; (3) 1 Corinthians 4:20; (4) Zechariah 4:6; (5) Acts 1:8; (6) Romans 1:16; (7) Ephesians 1:17; (8) Ephesians 1:18; (9) Ephesians 1:19; (10) Ephesians 1:20; (11) Ephesians 1:21; (12) Ephesians 3:20; (13) 2 Corinthians 2:14; (14) Ephesians 5:18; (15) Ephesians 6:10.

73

Praise

Key Thought: Praise belongs to God.

Key Scripture: *"From the rising of the sun to its going down the Lord's name is to be praised"* (Ps. 113:3, NKJV).

Letter From the Heart of God

Dear child, praise Me all day.[1] Give Me glory,[2] for this blesses Me.[3] Give thanks to Me.[4] Praise Me, for My mercy endures forever.[5]

Remember that My name is exalted above all blessing and praise.[6] Therefore, I beseech you, ascribe to Me glory and strength through your praise.[7] Give glory to My name and worship Me in the beauty of holiness.[8]

I will be exalted among the heathen, and I will be exalted in the earth.[9] My child, I am the King of all the earth; therefore, sing praises with understanding.[10] Open your lips and let your mouth show forth My praise.[11] This blesses Me, and it blesses you as well. Indeed, it is good to sing praises unto Me.[12]

Make a joyful noise unto Me.[13] Make known My deeds among the people.[14] Let everything that has breath praise Me.[15] My child, keep on praising Me. Call upon My name. Declare My doings among the people and proclaim that My name is exalted.[16]

My child, bless Me at all times and let My praise continually be in your mouth.[17] Let all that is within you bless My holy name. Remember all My benefits to you; I forgive all your iniquities, and I heal all your diseases. I redeem your life from destruction, and I crown you with My lovingkindness and tender mercies.[18]

You are a member of My chosen generation, a part of My royal priesthood and My holy nation, one of My very own people, whom I have called out of darkness into My glorious light.[19]

Therefore, continually offer to Me the sacrifice of praise, which is the fruit of your lips, thankfully acknowledging Me and giving glory to My name.[20]

With love and blessing,

Your faithful Father

References: (1) Psalms 113:3; (2) Joshua 7:19; (3) Psalms 68:35; (4) 2 Samuel 22:50; (5) 2 Chronicles 20:21; (6) Nehemiah 9:5; (7) Psalms 29:1; (8) Psalms 29:2; (9) Psalms 46:10; (10) Psalms 47:7; (11) Psalms 51:15; (12) Psalms 147:1; (13) Psalms 100:1; (14) Psalms 105:1; (15) Psalms 150:6; (16) Isaiah 12:4; (17) Psalms 34:1; (18) Psalms 103:1-4; (19) 1 Peter 2:9; (20) Hebrews 13:15.

74
Prayer

Key Thought: God hears and answers prayer.

Key Scripture: *"Call to Me, and I will answer you, and show you great and mighty things, which you do not know"* (Jer. 33:3, NKJV).

Letter From the Heart of God

My dear child, I want you to call to Me. Know that I will answer you and show you great and mighty things, which you do not know.[1] I will hear you when you call unto Me.[2] I do not forget the cry of the humble.[3] Lift up your soul to Me, My child.[4] Call upon Me in the day of trouble, and I will deliver you.[5]

When you pray to Me, I will answer you, and I promise to be with you in trouble.[6] I have inclined My ear unto you; therefore, be sure to call upon Me.[7] I promise to be near to you, when you call out to Me.[8] You shall seek Me and find Me, when you search for Me with all your heart.[9]

Pour out your heart like water before Me.[10] Call on My name, and I will hear you.[11] Always remember, My child, that I am your heavenly Father and I know the things you need even before you pray.[12] But, I want you to pray to Me. Ask, and it shall be given to you. Seek, and you shall find. Knock, and it shall be opened unto you.[13] This is My promise to you.

Be sure to abide in Jesus and let His words abide in you.[14] Then, whatsoever you ask for in prayer, believing, you shall receive.[15] And, whatever you ask Me in the name of Jesus, I will give you.[16] Always be led by the Holy Spirit in prayer,[17] for He will help you know how to pray and what to pray for.[18]

Your prayers are powerful and effective, for you are My righteous child in Christ. The effectual, fervent prayer of a righteous person always avails much, My child.[19] So, ask and receive, that your joy may be full.[20]

Rejoice evermore, My child. Pray without ceasing. In everything give thanks, for this is My will in Christ Jesus concerning you.[21]

Call unto Me,

Your heavenly Father

References: *(1) Jeremiah 33:3; (2) Psalms 4:3; (3) Psalms 9:12; (4) Psalms 25:1; (5) Psalms 50:15; (6) Psalms 91:15; (7) Psalms 116:2; (8) Psalms 145:18; (9) Jeremiah 29:13; (10) Lamentations 2:19; (11) Zechariah 13:9; (12) Matthew 6:8; (13) Matthew 7:7; (14) John 15:7; (15) Matthew 21:22; (16) John 16:23; (17) Romans 8:14; (18) Romans 8:26; (19) James 5:16; (20) John 16:24; (21) 1 Thessalonians 5:16-18.*

75

Pride

Key Thought: Pride has no place in a Christian's life.

Key Scripture: *"Pride goes before destruction, and a haughty spirit before a fall. Better to be of a humble spirit with the lowly, than to divide the spoil with the proud"* (Prov. 16:18-19, NKJV).

Letter From the Heart of God

Dearly beloved child, avoid all pride in your life, because pride goes before destruction and a haughty spirit goes before a fall.[1] Pride leads to shame, My child.[2] Be patient in spirit rather than proud.[3]

Do not glory in your own wisdom, might, or riches. Rather, glory in understanding and knowing Me, the Lord God, who exercises lovingkindness, judgment, and righteousness in the earth.[4] Whoever exalts himself shall be abased, and he who humbles himself shall be exalted.[5]

My child, do not love the world nor the things in the world. All that is in the world, the lust of the flesh, the lust of the eyes, the pride of life, is not of Me, but is of the world. The world and its lusts are passing away, but he who does My will abides forever.[6]

Humble yourself before Me, My child, because I resist the proud and give grace to the humble.[7] Whatever you do in word or deed, do it heartily as unto Me, not pridefully, for the praise of others.[8]

My child, humility must come before honor.[9] It is far better to be of a humble spirit with the lowly than it is to divide the spoil with the proud.[10] Blessed are the poor in spirit, for theirs is the kingdom of heaven.[11]

Always remember that without Jesus you can do nothing,[12] but through Him you can do all things.[13] My dear child, clothe yourself with humility.[14] It is good in My sight that you always do justly, love mercy, and walk humbly with Me.[15]

Trust in Me,

Your Father God

References: *(1) Proverbs 16:18-19; (2) Proverbs 11:2; (3) Ecclesiastes 7:8; (4) Jeremiah 9:24; (5) Matthew 23:12; (6) 1 John 2:15-17; (7) 1 Peter 5:5; (8) Colossians 3:17,23; (9) Proverbs 18:12; (10) Proverbs 16:19; (11) Matthew 5:3; (12) John 15:5; (13) Philippians 4:13; (14) 1 Peter 5:5; (15) Micah 6:8.*

Now you may wish to write a letter of personal response to God.

76

Promises of God

Key Thought: God always keeps His promises.

Key Scripture: *"By which have been given to us exceedingly great and precious promises, that through these you may be partakers of the divine nature, having escaped the corruption that is in the world through lust"* (2 Pet. 1:4, NKJV).

Letter From the Heart of God

Dear one, My exceedingly great and precious promises are for you. I have given you My promises, that through them you may become a partaker of My divine nature and escape the corruption that is in the world.[1] All My promises are yes and amen in Christ Jesus.[2] If you ask anything in His name, I will do it.[3]

My child, I am never slow about My promises, as some count slowness, but I am longsuffering toward you. I am not willing that anyone should perish but that all should come to repentance.[4]

My precious child, I want you to be an imitator of those who through faith and patience inherit My promises.[5] When you received My Son as your Savior, I began a good work in you, and I promise to continue it and bring it to perfect completion at the day of His return.[6]

Therefore, do not cast away your confidence, which has great reward. But exercise patient endurance, so that, when you have done My will, you may receive My promise.[7] Never forget that I am able to do exceedingly abundantly beyond all that you can ask or think, according to My power at work within you.[8]

Everyone who asks receives.[9] Therefore, My child, I want you to ask, knowing My promise that it shall be given you. Seek, and you shall find. Knock, and it shall be opened unto you.[10]

If an earthly father knows how to give good gifts to his children, how much more shall I, your heavenly Father, give good things to you when you ask Me?[11] I am rich unto all who call upon Me.[12] My eyes are over you, My child, and My ears are open to your prayers.[13]

Ask and receive that your joy may be full,[14] for I am the God of all hope and I will fill you with all joy and peace in believing, that you may abound in hope by the power of the Holy Spirit.[15]

All My love,

Your faithful Father

References: (1) 2 Peter 1:4; (2) 2 Corinthians 1:20; (3) John 14:14; (4) 2 Peter 3:9; (5) Hebrews 6:12; (6) Philippians 1:6; (7) Hebrews 10:35; (8) Ephesians 3:20; (9) Matthew 7:8; (10) Matthew 7:7; (11) Matthew 7:11; (12) Romans 10:12; (13) 1 Peter 3:12; (14) John 16:24; (15) Romans 15:13.

Now you may wish to write a letter of personal response to God.

77

Purity

Key Thought: Keep yourself pure.

Key Scripture: *"Blessed are the pure in heart: for they shall see God"* (Matt. 5:8).

Letter From the Heart of God

Dear child, keep yourself pure.[1] This will give you happiness, and it will enable you to see Me.[2] Who shall ascend My hill? Who shall stand in My holy place? It is he who has clean hands and a pure heart, he who has not lifted his soul unto vanity and has not sworn deceitfully.[3]

Remember that you are clean through the Word which I have spoken unto you.[4] You are the temple of My Holy Spirit, who lives and dwells within you. You are not your own; you were bought with a price.[5] Therefore, I want you to glorify Me in your body and in your spirit, which are Mine.[6]

I have called you unto holiness.[7] Therefore, draw near to Me, My child, and I will draw near to you. Cleanse your hands and purify your heart.[8]

Whatever is true, whatever is noble and honorable, whatever is right and just, whatever is pure, whatever is lovely, whatever is of good report, if there is anything virtuous and praiseworthy, think on these things.[9]

I want you to know, My child, that to the pure all things are pure, but to those who are defiled and unbelieving nothing is pure, but even their mind and their conscience are defiled.[10] As a newborn babe, desire the pure milk of My Word, that you may grow in all that My salvation means for you.[11]

You have been born again of incorruptible seed by My Word, which lives and abides forever.[12] As you purify your soul in obedience to My truth through the Spirit, see that you love others fervently, with a pure heart.[13]

Grace and peace to you,

Your heavenly Father

References: *(1) 1 Timothy 5:22; (2) Matthew 5:8; (3) Psalms 24:3-4; (4) John 15:3; (5) 1 Corinthians 6:19-20; (6) 1 Corinthians 6:20; (7) 1 Thessalonians 4:7; (8) James 4:8; (9) Philippians 4:8; (10) Titus 1:15; (11) 1 Peter 2:2; (12) 1 Peter 1:23; (13) 1 Peter 1:22.*

Now you may wish to write a letter of personal response to God.

78

Purpose

Key Thought: You were created to have fellowship with God.

Key Scripture: *"For we are His workmanship, created in Christ Jesus for good works, which God prepared beforehand that we should walk in them"* (Eph. 2:10, NKJV).

Letter From the Heart of God

My child, I created you with purpose, and My chief purpose and desire is that we might enjoy intimate fellowship.[1] Draw near to Me, and I will draw near to you.[2] I will always be with you, for I have promised never to leave you nor forsake you.[3]

I created you to be one with Me and with Jesus, as I am in Him and He in Me, that you may be one with Us and with your brothers and sisters in Christ. This unity and fellowship will also cause the world to know and believe that I sent Jesus to be their Savior.[4]

Therefore, with all believers, I have entrusted to you the ministry of reconciliation. You are an ambassador for Christ, called to beseech people in His behalf to be reconciled to Me.[5] As you minister in the mighty name of My Son, Jesus, remember that I have given you authority over all the power of the enemy, and nothing shall by any means hurt you.[6]

My child, before I formed you in the womb I knew you.[7] You are fearfully and wonderfully made. I saw your substance when I made you in secret and all of your days were written in My book before even one of them came to be.[8] I know the plans I have for you, plans for your good and not for evil, plans to give you a hope and a future.[9]

I have already prepared for you a unique purpose and good works for you to do.[10] You have a calling,[11] and I have endowed you with the spiritual gifts necessary for that calling,[12] which I will never take from you.[13] As your merciful and loving Father, I promise to comfort you in all your tribulations, so you will be able to comfort those who are in any trouble with the same comfort you have received from Me.[14]

I give only good gifts to My children,[15] so you can be certain My plans for you are perfect for your complete success and fulfillment. Therefore, I ask you to wait upon Me, for I want to show you my ways and teach you the path to accomplish My purpose for your life. I will lead you in the truth and teach you all you need to know to fulfill your purpose.[16]

Commit your way to Me, and I will bring to pass the purpose for your life. Delight yourself in Me, and I will give you the desires which I have placed in your heart.[17] Trust Me and do not lean to your own understanding. In all your ways acknowledge Me, and I will direct your paths to accomplish all that I have planned for you.[18]

Be encouraged, for I have great and wonderful things in store for you.

Walk in My wisdom,

Your devoted Father

References: *(1) 1 John 1:3; (2) James 4:8; (3) Hebrews 13:5; (4) John 17:21; (5) 2 Corinthians 5:18-20; (6) Luke 10:19; (7) Jeremiah 1:5; (8) Psalms 139:14-16; (9) Jeremiah 29:11; (10) Ephesians 2:10; (11) Ephesians 4:1; (12) Romans 12:6; (13) Romans 11:29; (14) 2 Corinthians 1:3-4; (15) James 1:17; (16) Psalms 25:4-5; (17) Psalms 37:4-5; (18) Proverbs 3:5-6.*

Now you may wish to write a letter of personal response to God.

79

Quietness

Key Thought: In quietness you will find strength.

Key Scripture: *"In returning and rest you shall be saved; in quietness and confidence shall be your strength"* (Isa. 30:15, NKJV).

Letter From the Heart of God

Dearly beloved, through quietness you will find confidence and strength.[1] I will keep you in perfect peace, if you keep your mind stayed on Me, because I know you trust Me.[2] Trust in Me forever, for I am your everlasting strength.[3]

Trust in Me with all your heart and do not lean unto your own understanding. In all your ways acknowledge Me, and I will direct your paths.[4]

Be still, and know that I am your God. I will be exalted among the nations. I will be exalted in the earth![5] Love truth and peace.[6]

Never forget that I am your Shepherd. Therefore, you shall want for nothing.[7] I will make you to lie down in green pastures, and I will lead you beside the still waters.[8] I will restore your soul, and lead you in the paths of righteousness for My name's sake.[9]

My child, remember that Jesus is your peace.[10] Seek peace and pursue it.[11] As a peace-maker, always sow in peace, and you will reap a harvest of righteousness.[12] The fruit of righteousness in your life shall be peace, and its effect is quietness and assurance forever.[13] Walk in quietness before Me, My child.

With love and peace,

Your heavenly Father

References: *(1) Isaiah 30:15; (2) Isaiah 26:3; (3) Isaiah 26:4; (4) Proverbs 3:5-6; (5) Psalms 46:10; (6) Zechariah 8:19; (7) Psalms 23:1; (8) Psalms 23:2; (9) Psalms 23:3; (10) Ephesians 2:14; (11) Psalms 34:14; (12) James 3:18; (13) Isaiah 32:17.*

Now you may wish to write a letter of personal response to God.

80

Redemption

Key Thought: Through faith in Christ you have been redeemed.

Key Scripture: *"And they sang a new song, saying: 'You are worthy to take the scroll, and to open its seals; for You were slain, and have redeemed us to God by Your blood out of every tribe and tongue and people and nation, and have made us kings and priests to our God; and we shall reign on the earth.'"* (Rev. 5:9-10, NKJV).

Letter From the Heart of God

My dear one, do not be ashamed of the Gospel of Christ, for it is My power for salvation to everyone who believes.[1] I have blessed you in heavenly places with every spiritual blessing in Christ, even as I chose you in Him before the foundation of the world, that you should be holy and without blame before Me.[2]

In love I predestined you to be My child, through Jesus Christ, which was according to the good pleasure of My will and is to the praise of My glorious grace, which I have freely bestowed upon you in My Beloved. In Christ you have redemption through His blood, the forgiveness of sins, according to the riches of My grace, which I have lavished upon you.[3]

211

Through My Son, Jesus Christ, I have redeemed you from the curse of the Law.[4] Because you are in Him, He has become for you wisdom, righteousness, sanctification, and redemption.[5]

My child, you are not your own, for you have been bought with a price.[6] You were not redeemed with perishable things, such as silver and gold, but with the precious blood of Christ, as of a lamb without spot or blemish.[7] You have been born again, not of perishable seed but of imperishable, by My living and eternal Word.[8]

Rejoice! Because you are in Christ, you are a new creation; old things have passed away and all things have become new.[9] I have delivered you from the power and dominion of darkness and I have brought you into the Kingdom of the Son of My love.[10]

My child, you are a member of My chosen generation, My royal priesthood, My holy nation, and My own special people, that you may proclaim My praises, for I have called you out of darkness, into My marvelous light.[11]

You have been crucified with Christ, and it is no longer you who lives, but it is Christ who lives in you; and the life you now live in the flesh you live by faith in My Son, who loved you and gave himself for you.[12] Therefore, sin shall no longer have dominion over you,[13] for you are dead and your life is hidden with Christ in Me.[14]

My child, you have been raised with Christ; therefore, seek those things that are above, where Christ is seated at My right hand.[15] Set your mind on things that are above and not on things that are on the earth.[16] When Christ who is your life appears, then you shall appear with Him in glory.[17]

As one of My redeemed, I want you to rejoice, pray without ceasing, and in everything give thanks, for this is My will in Christ Jesus concerning you.[18] I am the God of peace, and I will sanctify you wholly. I will preserve your whole spirit, soul, and body blameless at the coming of your Lord Jesus Christ. Remember, I have called you, I am faithful, and I will do it.[19]

Grace and peace to you,

God, your living Redeemer

References: (1) Romans 1:16; (2) Ephesians 1:3-4; (3) Ephesians 1:5-7; (4) Galatians 3:13; (5) 1 Corinthians 1:30; (6) 1 Corinthians 6:20; (7) 1 Peter 1:18-19; (8) 1 Peter 1:23; (9) 2 Corinthians 5:17; (10) Colossians 1:13; (11) 1 Peter 2:9; (12) Galatians 2:20; (13) Romans 6:14; (14) Colossians 3:3; (15) Colossians 3:1; (16) Colossians 3:2; (17) Colossians 3:4; (18) 1 Thessalonians 5:16-18; (19) 1 Thessalonians 5:23-24.

81

Responsibility

Key Thought: Your main responsibility is to respond to God's ability.

Key Scripture: *"He has shown you, O man, what is good; and what does the Lord require of you but to do justly, to love mercy, and to walk humbly with your God?"* (Mic. 6:8, NKJV).

Letter From the Heart of God

My dear child, I am so happy that you have received Jesus Christ as your personal Savior and Lord.[1] As a born-again believer[2] you have been delivered from the power of darkness and brought into the Kingdom of the Son of My love.[3]

My kingdom cannot be shaken, and, as a child of My kingdom, express your gratitude by serving Me with reverence and awe.[4]

I beseech you, by My mercies to you, that you present your body a living sacrifice, holy and acceptable to Me, which is your reasonable service of worship.[5] And do not be conformed to this world, but be transformed by the renewing of your mind, that you may prove what is My good, acceptable, and perfect will for you.[6]

Study and do your best to present yourself to Me as one approved, a worker who does not need to be ashamed and who correctly handles My Word of truth.[7] Remember that My Word is alive and powerful, and it is able to discern the thoughts and intents of your heart.[8]

My Word will always be a lamp to your feet and a light unto your path.[9] Therefore, be careful to walk in the light of My Word at all times.[10]

Do all you can to maintain the unity with other believers in the bond of peace.[11] In humility of mind, have compassion for others, loving them, and always being tender-hearted and courteous toward them.[12] Indeed, this is what I require of you, that you would do justly, love mercy, and walk humbly with Me.[13]

Refrain your tongue from evil and your lips from speaking deceit. Turn away from evil and do good. Seek peace and pursue it, remembering that My eyes are upon you and My ears are open to your prayers.[14]

Pursue righteousness, godliness, faith, love, patience, and gentleness. Fight the good fight of faith, lay hold on eternal life, to which you were called and have confessed the good confession in the presence of many witnesses.[15]

Be filled continually with the Holy Spirit,[16] and let the fruit of the Holy Spirit work in and through you, causing you to show forth love, joy, peace, patience, gentleness, meekness, and self-control.[17]

The Spirit of life in Christ Jesus has set you free from the law of sin and death.[18] Stand fast in the liberty wherewith Christ has made you free and don't be entangled again with any yoke of bondage.[19]

Be renewed in the spirit of your mind and put on the new self, which has been created to be like Me in true righteousness and holiness.[20] Be holy in all that you do, for I am holy.[21]

Be angry and do not sin. Do not let the sun go down on your anger, nor give any place to the devil.[22] Humble yourself under My mighty hand,[23] and submit yourself to Me. Resist the devil, and he will flee from you. Draw near to Me, and I will draw near to you.[24]

Be My follower, dear child, and walk in love, as Christ has loved you and given himself for you.[25] Remember that I am always with you to help you fulfill every responsibility of your life.[26]

I am with you always,

Your heavenly Father

References: *(1) Romans 10:9-10; (2) 1 Peter 1:23; (3) Colossians 1:13; (4) Hebrews 12:28; (5) Romans 12:1; (6) Romans 12:2; (7) 1 Timothy 2:15; (8) Hebrews 4:12; (9) Psalms 119:105; (10) 1 John 1:7; (11) Ephesians 4:3; (12) 1 Peter 3:8; (13) Micah 6:8; (14) 1 Peter 3:10-12; (15) 1 Timothy 6:11-12; (16) Ephesians 5:18; (17) Galatians 5:22-23; (18) Romans 8:2; (19) Galatians 5:1; (20) Ephesians 4:24; (21) 1 Peter 1:16; (22) Ephesians 4:26-27; (23) 1 Peter 5:6; (24) James 4:7-8; (25) Ephesians 5:1-2; (26) Hebrews 13:5.*

Now you may wish to write a letter of personal response to God.

82

Righteousness

Key Thought: Righteousness is a gift from God.

Key Scripture: *"For He made Him who knew no sin to be sin for us that we might become the righteousness of God in Him"* (2 Cor. 5:21, NKJV).

Letter From the Heart of God

My greatly loved child, I am writing to you about righteousness, because I want you to understand it more fully and to experience it more completely. Simply stated, righteousness does not come to you through your obedience to the Law;[1] rather it is a gift I've given to you through faith in My Son, Jesus Christ,[2] who is the Righteous One.[3] In fact, you cannot make yourself righteous at all, for all of your righteousness is as filthy rags in My sight.[4]

It is those who receive the abundance of My grace and the free gift of righteousness who will reign in life through Christ Jesus.[5] He is ever and always, the Lord, your righteousness.[6]

Because I love you so much, I made Jesus Christ, who knew no sin, to be sin for you, that you would become My righteousness in Him.[7] My child, Jesus is My sacrificial lamb, who takes away the sins of the world.[8] Jesus died for you, to take your sins from you, and your old self was crucified with Him, that the body of sin might be done away with and you would no longer be a slave to sin.[9]

Since you have died with Christ, you have been freed from sin, and now you are alive with Him. Therefore, knowing that Christ, having been raised from the dead, dies no more, death no longer has dominion over Him.[10]

When Jesus died for you, He died to sin once for all, and the life He lives, He lives to Me. This is what I want for you also, My child. Therefore, reckon yourself to be dead to sin, but alive to Me in Christ Jesus, your Lord.[11] Present all your members and faculties as servants of righteousness for holiness and sanctification.[12]

Now you are able to be filled with the fruits of righteousness, which are by Jesus Christ, to My praise and glory.[13] Indeed, it is My doing that you are in Christ Jesus, whom I have made to be your wisdom, righteousness, sanctification, and redemption.[14] Rejoice! For the law of the Spirit of life in Christ Jesus has freed you from the law of sin and death.[15]

Now, therefore, My child, I remind you that you have been crucified with Christ. Because this is true, it is no longer you who lives, but it is Christ who lives in you, and the life which you now live in the flesh you live by faith in My Son, who loved you and gave His life for you.[16]

Keep remembering that righteousness only comes by faith in Christ.[17] So, please, My child, walk by faith and not by sight.[18] You can do all things through Christ who strengthens you.[19]

Be continually filled with the Holy Spirit[20] and remember to walk after the Spirit and not after the lusts of the flesh.[21] Walk in righteousness before Me, My child. As you do so, I will withhold no good thing from you.[22]

Now, do you see the great benefits and rewards of righteousness in your life, My child?[23] Keep on keeping on, and let My righteousness flow from your life and everywhere you go.

With constant love,

God, your Father

References: *(1) Philippians 3:9; (2) Romans 5:17; (3) 1 John 2:1; (4) Isaiah 64:6; (5) Romans 5:17; (6) Jeremiah 23:6; (7) 2 Corinthians 5:21; (8) John 1:29; (9) Romans 6:5-6; (10) Romans 6:7-9; (11) Romans 6:10-11; (12) Romans 6:19; (13) Philippians 1:11; (14) 1 Corinthians 1:30; (15) Romans 8:2; (16) Galatians 2:20; (17) Philippians 3:9; (18) 2 Corinthians 5:7; (19) Philippians 4:13; (20) Ephesians 5:18; (21) Galatians 5:16; (22) Psalms 84:11; (23) Psalms 58:11.*

83

Service to God and Others

Key Thought: To love God is to serve Him and others.

Key Scripture: *"Serve the Lord with gladness: come before His presence with singing"* (Ps. 100:2).

Letter From the Heart of God

My dear, precious child, serve Me with gladness, and come before My presence with singing.[1] Make a joyful shout to Me.[2] Know that I am the Lord, your God, and I am your Creator.[3] Serve Me with all your heart and soul.[4] Serve Me with a perfect heart and a willing mind.[5] Minister to Me.[6]

Serve Me and others in newness of spirit and not in the oldness of the letter.[7] I have called you to liberty, My child, but do not use that liberty as an opportunity to serve your flesh, but through love serve one another.[8] Remember that all the Law is fulfilled in one word, even in this: "You shall love your neighbor as yourself."[9]

Bear the burdens of others, and so fulfill the law of Christ.[10] Do not allow yourself to grow weary while doing good, for in due season you shall reap, if you do not lose heart.[11]

Therefore, My child, as you have opportunity, do good to all, especially to those who are of the household of faith.[12]

Grace and peace be yours,

Your loving Father

References: *(1) Psalms 100:2; (2) Psalms 100:1; (3) Psalms 100:3; (4) Deuteronomy 10:12; (5) 1 Chronicles 28:9; (6) Acts 13:2; (7) Romans 7:6; (8) Galatians 5:13; (9) Galatians 5:14; (10) Galatians 6:2; (11) Galatians 6:9; (12) Galatians 6:10.*

Now you may wish to write a letter of personal response to God.

84

Sin

Key Thought: Sin separates you from God and others.

Key Scripture: *"Where sin abounded, grace did much more abound"* (Rom. 5:20).

Letter From the Heart of God

My child, I want to assure you that My grace is greater than any and all sin.[1] I want you to avoid all sin, but if you do sin, always remember that you have an Advocate with Me, who is Jesus Christ, the Righteous One.[2] He is your Counselor.[3] When He pleads your case before Me, it is never possible for Satan, your adversary[4] and accuser[5] to prevail, for Jesus is the sacrifice for your sins.[6]

Walk in the light as He is in the light; then, you will have fellowship with Me, Jesus, and your fellow-believers, and the blood of Jesus Christ will cleanse you from all sin.[7] If you confess your sins, I will be faithful and just to forgive you of your sins and to cleanse you from all unrighteousness.[8]

My child, sin shall not have dominion over you, for you are not under the Law. You are under grace.[9] Never forget that the wages of sin is death, but My gift to you is eternal life through Jesus Christ, your Lord.[10] Therefore, make no provision for the flesh, to fulfill its lusts.[11]

Whatsoever is not of faith is sin.[12] Christ died for your sins.[13] Therefore, I implore you to awake to righteousness and sin not.[14] Having been justified by Christ, live by faith,[15] through placing your absolute trust in My Word,[16] My promises,[17] and My faithfulness.[18]

Keep on abiding in Christ, and do not sin, My beloved child.[19]

With love and grace,

Your faithful Father

References: (1) Romans 5:20; (2) 1 John 2:1; (3) Isaiah 9:6; (4) 1 Peter 5:8; (5) Revelation 12:10; (6) 1 John 2:2; (7) 1 John 1:7; (8) 1 John 1:9; (9) Romans 6:14; (10) Romans 6:23; (11) Romans 13:14; (12) Romans 14:23; (13) 1 Corinthians 15:3; (14) 1 Corinthians 15:34; (15) Romans 1:17; (16) Romans 10:17; (17) 2 Corinthians 1:20; (18) Hebrews 10:23; (19) 1 John 3:6.

Now you may wish to write a letter of personal response to God.

85

Sorrow

Key Thought: God knows all about your sorrows.

Key Scripture: *"Most assuredly, I say to you that you will weep and lament, but the world will rejoice; and you will be sorrowful, but your sorrow will be turned into joy"* (John 16:20, NKJV).

Letter From the Heart of God

Dearly loved child, I will turn your sorrow into joy.[1] It is My delight to be able to heal those who are heartbroken, and I have the power to bind up all their wounds.[2] Do not let the sorrow of your heart break your spirit, My child.[3]

Never forget that My Son, Jesus, is familiar with sorrow and acquainted with grief.[4] He understands your sorrow,[5] but be of good cheer, because He has overcome the world.[6]

My child, remember that My blessing in your life makes you rich, and I will add no sorrow with it.[7] Let your sorrow lead you to repentance, for godly sorrow produces repentance that leads to salvation, but the sorrow of the world produces death.[8]

Remember that I am the Father of mercies and the God of all comfort.[9] Receive My

comfort for your sorrow, My child, for I am
your shield, your glory, and the lifter of your
head.[10] Fear not, for I am with you,[11] and I will
bless and comfort you.[12]

> With tender love,
>
> *Your caring Father*

References: *(1) John 16:20; (2) Psalms 147:3; (3) Proverbs
15:13; (4) Isaiah 53:3; (5) Hebrews 4:15; (6) John 16:33;
(7) Proverbs 10:22; (8) 2 Corinthians 7:9-10; (9) 2
Corinthians 1:3; (10) Psalms 3:3; (11) Hebrews 13:5; (12)
Matthew 5:4.*

*Now you may wish to write a letter of personal
response to God.*

86

Speech

Key Thought: Be slow to speak.

Key Scripture: *"And whatever you do in word or deed, do all in the name of the Lord Jesus, giving thanks to God the Father through Him"* (Col. 3:17, NKJV).

Letter From the Heart of God

Dearly beloved, whatever you do in word or deed, do all in the name of your Lord Jesus Christ, giving thanks to Me through Him.[1] Hide My Word in your heart that you might not sin against Me,[2] for out of the abundance of your heart your mouth will speak.[3]

Remember that death and life are in the power of the tongue[4] and the potential for sin lurks in an unnecessary multitude of words.[5] Therefore, be swift to hear, but slow to speak and slow to wrath.[6] My child, a soft answer turns away wrath.[7]

Let the words of your mouth and the meditations of your heart be acceptable in My sight, for I am your strength and your Redeemer.[8] Speak truth with your neighbor,[9] and always speak the truth in love.[10] An appropriate word that you speak in due season is very good, indeed.[11]

Pleasant words are as a honeycomb, sweet to the soul and health to the body.[12] Do not be rash with your mouth, My child.[13] Let no evil or unwholesome speech come out of your mouth, but only such as is good for edification and imparts grace to those who hear.[14]

Let your speech be always with grace, seasoned with salt, that you may know how you ought to answer the questions others present to you.[15] In order to love life, My child, and to see good days, be sure to refrain your tongue from all evil.[16]

Therefore, do not be unwise, but understand My will. Be continually filled with the Holy Spirit, speaking in psalms and hymns, and spiritual songs, singing and making melody in your heart unto Me. Always and for everything give thanks to Me in the name of your Lord Jesus Christ.[17]

With all My love,

Your heavenly Father

References: (1) Colossians 3:17; (2) Psalms 119:11; (3) Matthew 12:34; (4) Proverbs 18:21; (5) Proverbs 10:19; (6) James 1:19; (7) Proverbs 15:1; (8) Psalms 19:14; (9) Ephesians 4:25; (10) Ephesians 4:15; (11) Proverbs 15:23; (12) Proverbs 16:24; (13) Ecclesiastes 5:2; (14) Ephesians 4:29; (15) Colossians 4:6; (16) 1 Peter 3:10; (17) Ephesians 5:17-20.

87

Strength

Key Thought: God is the source of your strength.

Key Scripture: *"Be strong in the Lord and in the power of His might"* (Eph. 6:10, NKJV).

Letter From the Heart of God

Dearly beloved, always remember your strength is in Me. It is My might that empowers you.[1] You can do all things through Christ who strengthens you.[2] In quietness and confidence in Me shall be your strength.[3]

I am your strength and your song.[4] My joy is your strength.[5] Be strong in Me, therefore, My child.[6] I delight in being your strength and your shield.[7] My way is strength for you at all times.[8] Let My wisdom strengthen you,[9] and remember that My wisdom is even better than strength.[10]

Trust in Me, My child, for in Me you will always find everlasting strength.[11] Wisdom and strength belong to Me.[12] It is not through human might or power that you will accomplish anything, but it is through My Spirit alone.[13] My strength is made perfect in your weakness, for My grace shall always be sufficient for you.[14]

I want you to know, My child, that I am
your Rock, your fortress, and your Deliverer. I
am your God, your strength, your shield, the
horn of your salvation, and your stronghold.
Therefore, trust in Me and call upon Me; in
this way you will be strengthened and saved
from all your enemies.[15]

Be strong in Me and in the grace that is in
Christ Jesus,[16] for I love you, My child.

Grace and strength to you,

Your almighty Father

References: *(1) Ephesians 6:10; (2) Philippians 4:13; (3)
Isaiah 30:15; (4) Exodus 15:2; (5) Nehemiah 8:10; (6) 1
Kings 2:2; (7) Psalms 28:7; (8) Proverbs 10:29; (9)
Ecclesiastes 7:19; (10) Ecclesiastes 9:16; (11) Isaiah 26:4;
(12) Daniel 2:20; (13) Zechariah 4:6; (14) 2 Corinthians
12:9; (15) Psalms 18:1-3; (16) 2 Timothy 2:1.*

*Now you may wish to write a letter of personal
response to God.*

88

Success

Key Thought: God measures success with a different standard from that of the world.

Key Scripture: *"If the ax is dull, and one does not sharpen the edge, then he must use more strength; but wisdom brings success"* (Eccles. 10:10, NKJV).

Letter From the Heart of God

My special child, remember that wisdom will bring success to you.[1] If you lack wisdom, ask Me for it, and I will give it to you liberally and without reproach. Be sure, however, that you ask in faith, with no doubting. He who doubts is like a wave of the sea that is driven and tossed by the wind.[2] If you doubt and are double-minded, you will be unstable in all your ways and will not be able to receive anything from Me.

The faith I give you is the substance of the things you hope for and the evidence of the things you do not yet see.[3] Faith comes to you as you hear My Word,[4] so feed on My Word and your faith will grow exceedingly.[5] Be strong in faith, giving glory to Me, being fully persuaded that, what I have promised, I am able and willing to perform in your life.[6]

Be strong and of good courage, My child.[7] Be a doer of the Word, and not a hearer only,[8] being sure to do according to all that you find therein. Do not turn from it to the right hand or to the left, for then you will prosper wherever you go.[9]

Do not let My Word depart from your mouth, but meditate on it day and night, so that you may observe to do according to all that is written in it, for then you will make your way prosperous and then you will have good success.[10]

It is My desire to make you the head, and not the tail. You shall be above only, and not beneath.[11] As you trust and believe in Me, My child, you shall be established and you shall prosper.[12] As long as you seek Me, I will make sure you prosper.[13] Seek first My kingdom and My righteousness, and I will supply all your needs.[14]

Commit your works unto Me, My child, and your thoughts shall be established.[15] Delight yourself in My Word and meditate in My Word day and night. When you do this, you shall become like a tree that is planted by the rivers of water. You will be fruitful, and whatever you do will prosper.[16]

Every good blessing,

Your faithful Father

References: *(1) Ecclesiastes 10:10; (2) James 1:5-6; (3) Hebrews 11:1; (4) Romans 10:17; (5) 2 Thessalonians 1:3; (6) Romans 4:20; (7) Joshua 1:6; (8) James 1:22; (9) Joshua 1:7; (10) Joshua 1:8; (11) Deuteronomy 28:13; (12) 2 Chronicles 20:20; (13) 2 Chronicles 26:5; (14) Matthew 6:33; (15) Proverbs 16:3; (16) Psalms 1.*

Now you may wish to write a letter of personal response to God.

89

Temptation

Key Thought: Do not yield to temptation, for yielding is sin.

Key Scripture: *"Watch and pray, lest you enter into temptation. The spirit indeed is willing, but the flesh is weak"* (Matt. 26:41, NKJV).

Letter From the Heart of God

My dear child, watch and pray at all times. This will prevent you from falling into temptation.[1] Take heed to yourself, so your heart will not be deceived.[2] Keep on walking in your integrity, My child.[3]

If sinners entice you, do not give consent to them.[4] Remember that discretion shall preserve you and understanding will keep you.[5]

Yield yourself totally to Me, My child.[6] Put on all of the armor I've provided for you, so that you will be able to stand against the wiles of the devil.[7] Be strong in Me, and in the power of My might.[8] Submit yourself to Me. Resist the devil, and he will flee from you.[9] Draw near to Me, and I will draw near to you.[10]

My Word is alive and powerful and is a discerner of the very thoughts and intents of your heart.[11] Take heed to My Word,[12] therefore, and hide it in your heart, so you will not sin against Me.[13]

I know how to deliver you from all temptations that may come your way, My child.[14] Remember, My Son, Jesus, was tempted in all things, just as you are, but did not sin. He is now your High Priest and understands your weaknesses and temptations.[15] Be encouraged, My child, for you can overcome all temptations and do all things through Christ, who strengthens you.[16]

Realize that no temptation comes to you which is not common to all people, but I promise to be faithful to you, and I will make a way of escape, so that you will be able to endure it.[17] Blessed are you when you patiently endure temptation, for, when you have stood the test, you will receive the crown of life, which I have promised to those who love Me.[18]

Trust in Me,

Your faithful Father

References: *(1) Matthew 26:41; (2) Deuteronomy 11:16; (3) Psalms 26:11; (4) Proverbs 1:10; (5) Proverbs 2:11; (6) Romans 6:13; (7) Ephesians 6:11-18; (8) Ephesians 6:10; (9) James 4:7; (10) James 4:8; (11) Hebrews 4:12; (12) Psalms 119:9; (13) Psalms 119:11; (14) 2 Peter 2:9; (15) Hebrews 4:15; (16) Philippians 4:13; (17) 1 Corinthians 10:13; (18) James 1:12.*

90
Trust

Key Thought: God is worthy of all your trust.

Key Scripture: *"Trust in the Lord with all your heart, and lean not on your own understanding; in all your ways acknowledge Him, and He shall direct your paths"* (Prov. 3:5-6, NKJV).

Letter From the Heart of God

My dear child, trust in Me with all your heart. Do not lean on your own understanding. Instead, lean on Me, and acknowledge Me in all your ways. As you do this, I promise to direct your paths.[1]

Keep your eyes upon Me.[2] As you place your trust in Me, rejoice,[3] for trusting Me will bring you blessing and happiness.[4] I am your Rock and your fortress. I am your Deliverer, your God, your strength. Trust in Me, My child.[5]

Commit your way to Me, as you trust in Me.[6] Trust in Me forever, for I am your everlasting strength.[7] Believe Me, My child, it is far better to trust in Me than to put your confidence in people.[8]

If you ask anything according to My will, I will hear you, and you can be confident that, if I hear your request, you will have what you asked of Me.[9] Therefore, place your faith and trust in Me, knowing that, whatever you ask in prayer, believing, you shall receive.[10] You can count on that, My child, because I am neither slack nor late in keeping My promises.[11]

My divine power has given you everything you need for life and godliness.[12] You can trust My exceedingly great and precious promises, which enable you to partake of My very nature, having escaped the corruption that is in the world through lust.[13] Trust Me at all times, My precious child.

Rely on me,

Your devoted Father

References: *(1) Proverbs 3:5-6; (2) 2 Chronicles 20:12; (3) Psalms 5:11; (4) Psalms 2:12; (5) Psalms 18:2; (6) Psalms 37:5; (7) Isaiah 26:4; (8) Psalms 118:8; (9) 1 John 5:14-15; (10) Matthew 21:22; (11) 2 Peter 3:9; (12) 2 Peter 1:3; (13) 2 Peter 1:4.*

Now you may wish to write a letter of personal response to God.

91
Truth

Key Thought: Knowing God's truth will make you free.

Key Scripture: *"I have no greater joy than to hear that my children walk in truth"* (3 John 4).

Letter From the Heart of God

My beloved child, it gives Me great joy to know that you are walking in truth.[1] Love both truth and peace.[2] Always remember that My truth endures forever.[3] I sanctify you through My truth. My Word is truth.[4] It has been true from the beginning.[5] Heaven and earth shall pass away, but My Word will never pass away.[6]

The Law was given by Moses, but grace and truth came by Jesus Christ.[7] In fact, He is the way, the truth, and the life, and no one can come to Me, unless they do so through Him.[8]

Abide in My Word, and abide in Christ, then you will be His disciple, and you will know the truth which will make you free.[9] Jesus came to bear witness to the truth.[10] The truth is in Jesus.[11]

Also, My child, remember that I have given you the Holy Spirit, the Spirit of truth, to lead you into all truth.[12] Therefore, think on whatsoever things are true, honest, just, pure, lovely, and of good report,[13] and remember that I will never lie to you, My child.[14] Therefore, you, too, must speak the truth always[15] and speak it in love, so you may grow up in every way into union with Christ.[16]

Walk in My truth,

Your loving Father

References: (1) 3 John 4; (2) Zechariah 8:19; (3) Psalms 117:2; (4) John 17:17; (5) Psalms 119:160; (6) Matthew 24:35; (7) John 1:17; (8) John 14:6; (9) John 8:31-32; (10) John 18:37; (11) Ephesians 4:21; (12) John 16:13; (13) Philippians 4:8; (14) Numbers 23:19; (15) Ephesians 4:25; (16) Ephesians 4:15.

Now you may wish to write a letter of personal response to God.

92

Victory

Key Thought: You are a victor in Christ.

Key Scripture: *"But thanks be to God, who gives us the victory through our Lord Jesus Christ"* (1 Cor. 15:57, NKJV).

Letter From the Heart of God

My dear child, I have already given you the victory through your Lord Jesus Christ.[1] Sing unto Me, for I always triumph gloriously.[2] My right hand is glorious in power, and I dash My enemies to pieces.[3]

I am fighting in your behalf.[4] I favor you, My child, and I will not let your enemies triumph over you.[5] In fact, I will make sure that your enemies lick the dust.[6]

I have given you authority over all the power of the enemy and nothing shall by any means hurt you.[7] I resist the proud and give grace to the humble. Therefore, submit yourself to Me, resist the devil, and he will flee from you.[8]

Be of good cheer, for Jesus has overcome the world.[9] Likewise, because you have been born of Me, you overcome the world. And this is the victory that overcomes the world, even your faith.[10] You are an overcomer, My child, because greater am I in you than he that is in the world.[11] So, be strong in Me and in the power of My might.[12]

In everything, My child, you shall be more than a conqueror through Jesus, who loves you.[13] Always remember that nothing shall ever be able to separate you from My love, which is in Christ Jesus, your Lord.[14]

Remember that I am able to give you complete victory in every situation, because Mine is the greatness, the power, the glory, the victory, and the majesty. All that is in heaven and on earth is Mine. Riches and honor come from Me, and I reign over all. In My hand is power and might, the power to make great and to give strength to all.[15]

Believe all the promises of My Word, dear one, and you shall enjoy great victory indeed.

In victorious love,

Your heavenly Father

References: *(1) 1 Corinthians 15:57; (2) Exodus 15:1; (3) Exodus 15:6; (4) Joshua 23:10; (5) Psalms 41:11; (6) Psalms 72:9; (7) Luke 10:19; (8) James 4:6-7; (9) John 16:33; (10) 1 John 5:4; (11) 1 John 4:4; (12) Ephesians 6:10; (13) Romans 8:37; (14) Romans 8:38-39; (15) 1 Chronicles 29:11-13.*

93

Wisdom

Key Thought: Wisdom is a very precious commodity.

Key Scripture: *"Wisdom is the principal thing; therefore get wisdom. And in all your getting, get understanding"* (Prov. 4:7, NKJV).

Letter From the Heart of God

My dear child, always remember that wisdom is the principal thing. Therefore, get wisdom and understanding.[1] Wisdom is more precious than rubies, and all the things you desire cannot be compared with it. In wisdom is found length of days, riches, and honor. The ways of wisdom are pleasant and all its paths are peace. Wisdom is a tree of life to all who lay hold of it, and retaining wisdom will bring you happiness and blessing.[2]

I founded the earth by wisdom, and I established the heavens by understanding. My child, keep sound wisdom and discretion; they will be life to your soul and an adornment to your neck. Then you will walk safely along your way, and your foot will not stumble. When you lie down, you will not be afraid; you will lie down, and your sleep will be sweet.[3]

Hold your peace, and I will teach you My wisdom.[4] Reverence for Me is the beginning of wisdom in your life, My child.[5] I love to give wisdom. From My mouth you will receive wisdom, knowledge, and understanding.[6] The wisdom I give you is first pure, peaceable, gentle, willing to yield, full of mercy and good fruits, without partiality and without hypocrisy.[7]

Therefore, when you need wisdom, ask Me for it, and I will give it to you. Be sure you ask in faith, without doubting, and you shall have it.[8]

For all these reasons, My beloved, I want you to seek wisdom from Me, remembering that wisdom and might are Mine.[9]

Blessings and wisdom to you,

Your heavenly Father

References: (1) Proverbs 4:7; (2) Proverbs 3:14-18; (3) Proverbs 3:19-24; (4) Job 33:33; (5) Psalms 111:10; (6) Proverbs 2:6; (7) James 3:17; (8) James 1:5-6; (9) Daniel 2:20.

Now you may wish to write a letter of personal response to God.

94

Work

Key Thought: Work is a gift of God.

Key Scripture: *"I know that nothing is better for them than to rejoice, and to do good in their lives, and also that every man should eat and drink and enjoy the good of all his labor – it is the gift of God"* (Eccles. 3:12-13, NKJV).

Letter From the Heart of God

My dear child, enjoy your work and enjoy the fruits of your labor, for they are My gift to you.[1] Rejoice before Me in all that you set your hand to do.[2] Your diligence will lead you to prosperity.[3] When you work hard you shall be blessed.[4] In all labor there is profit, My child.[5]

Commit your works to Me, and your thoughts shall be established.[6] Remember, you are My workmanship, created in Christ Jesus unto good works that I have ordained for you to do.[7] Seek Me for your purpose,[8] for when you walk in the works I have ordained, great will be your joy[9] and your success.[10]

Whatever your hand finds to do, do it with all your might.[11] And whatever you do, do it heartily, as doing it for Me, and not for the praise or approval of others.[12] You are a laborer together with Me, My child.[13] Do everything heartily, as unto Me.[14] You will receive the reward of the inheritance, as you serve the Lord Christ in all that you do.[15]

My child, study to show yourself approved unto Me, a worker who never needs to be ashamed, because you know how to rightly divide My Word.[16] Whatever you do in word or deed, do all in the name of the Lord Jesus, giving thanks to Me through Him.[17]

Lovingly,

God, your Father

References: *(1) Ecclesiastes 3:12-13; (2) Deuteronomy 12:18; (3) Proverbs 10:4; (4) Proverbs 13:11; (5) Proverbs 14:23; (6) Proverbs 16:3; (7) Ephesians 2:10; (8) Ephesians 3:11; (9) Ecclesiastes 3:22; (10) Joshua 1:8; (11) Ecclesiastes 9:10; (12) 1 Corinthians 10:31; (13) 1 Corinthians 3:9; (14) Colossians 3:23; (15) Colossians 3:24; (16) 2 Timothy 2:15; (17) Colossians 3:17.*

Now you may wish to write a letter of personal response to God.

95
Worry

Key Thought: Worrying is like a rocking chair. It gives you something to do, but it doesn't get you anywhere.

Key Scripture: *"Cast your burden on the Lord, and He shall sustain you; He shall never permit the righteous to be moved"* (Ps. 55:22, NKJV).

Letter From the Heart of God

My dear child, I invite you to cast your burdens on Me. As you do so, I promise to sustain you.[1] Indeed, I want you to cast all your cares upon Me, because I care for you.[2] Pour out your heart before Me, because I am your refuge.[3] Seek first My kingdom and My righteousness, and I promise to supply your needs.[4]

Don't let your heart be troubled, neither let it be afraid.[5] Jesus gives you His peace. It is a peace that the world cannot give nor receive.[6] Remember that your worries have the power to choke the truth of My Word in your life.[7] Replace your worries with the truth of My Word, for My word is truth,[8] and your worries are lies of the enemy.[9]

Never forget that the enemy comes to steal, kill and destroy, but Jesus came to give you abundant life.[10] Take the shield of faith with which you will be able to quench all the fiery darts of the enemy, including worry, and take the helmet of salvation, which protects your mind, and the sword of the Spirit, which is My Word.[11] The faith My Word imparts to you[12] will give you the victory over every worry.[13]

My child, the weapons of this warfare are not carnal, but they are mighty through Me for pulling down strongholds, casting down imaginations and arguments and every high thing that exalts itself against the knowledge of Me and My care for you. The way to win the battle against worry is to bring every one of your thoughts and worries into captivity, making them obedient to Christ and My Word.[14]

Above all things, My child, put on love, which is the bond of perfection.[15] Let My peace rule in your heart, to which I have called you, and be thankful.[16]

When you are tempted to worry, don't do it. Don't ever worry about anything. Instead, by prayer and supplication, with thanksgiving, let your requests be made known to Me. When you do this, My peace, which surpasses all understanding, will guard your heart and mind through Christ Jesus.[17]

Have faith in Me,[18] remembering that I will keep you in perfect peace when you keep your mind stayed on Me, because you trust in

Me.[19] So, trust Me instead of worrying, My child.

I'm always with you,

Your Abba Father

References: *(1) Psalms 55:22; (2) 1 Peter 5:7; (3) Psalms 62:8; (4) Matthew 6:33; (5) John 14:1; (6) John 14:27; (7) Matthew 13:22; (8) John 17:17; (9) John 8:44; (10) John 10:10; (11) Ephesians 6:16-17; (12) Romans 10:17; (13) 1 John 5:4; (14) 1 Corinthians 10:4-5; (15) Colossians 3:14; (16) Colossians 3:15; (17) Philippians 4:6-7; (18) Mark 11:22; (19) Isaiah 26:3.*

Now you may wish to write a letter of personal response to God.

96

Worship

Key Thought: God is worthy of your worship.

Key Scripture: *"You shall worship the Lord your God, and Him only you shall serve"* (Matt. 4:10, NKJV).

Letter From the Heart of God

My beloved child, the hour is coming and now is, when the true worshipers will worship Me in spirit and in truth, for I seek such to worship Me. Remember that I am Spirit, and those who worship Me must worship Me in spirit and in truth.[1] I want you to worship Me, because worship will enable you to have intimate fellowship with Me.[2]

I will show you the path of life, and, through worship, you will discover that there is fullness of joy in My presence and at My right hand there are pleasures forevermore.[3] My child, please worship and serve Me alone.[4]

As you know, I love you with an everlasting love. Therefore, with lovingkindness I am drawing you close to Me.[5] Draw near to Me, and I will draw near to you.[6]

The thoughts I think toward you, My child, are thoughts of good and not of evil, to give you a future and a hope. I invite you, therefore, to call upon Me and pray to Me, and I assure you that I will listen to you. And you will seek Me and find Me, when you search for Me with all your heart.[7]

Worship will enable you to do this; therefore, I want you to love Me with all your heart, soul, and might.[8] Serve Me and worship Me with all your heart and soul.[9] Worship and bow down before Me, My child, and kneel before Me, for I am your Creator.[10]

Make a joyful noise to Me and serve Me with gladness. Come before My presence with singing and fully know and realize who I am, the Lord God who created you. Remember that I made you, and you are My child and a sheep in My pasture. With this realization in mind, be sure to worship Me by entering My gates with thanksgiving and coming into My courts with praise. Be thankful to Me and bless My name, for I am good; My mercy is ever-lasting and My truth endures to all generations.[11] Don't these truths fill your heart with a desire to worship Me?

Worship Me, My child, in the beauty of holiness.[12] Honor and majesty are before Me, and strength and beauty are in My sanctuary.[13]

Oh, give thanks to Me and call upon My name. Make My deeds known among the people! Sing to Me; sing psalms to Me. Talk of all My wondrous works and glory in My holy name. Let your heart rejoice, as you seek and worship Me. Seek Me and My strength. Seek My face forevermore.[14] As you worship Me, remember My marvelous works and wonders.[15]

I am the Rock of your salvation. Therefore, shout joyfully to Me. Come before My presence with thanksgiving. Sing psalms to Me with joy. As you worship Me in this way, you will know that I am your great God, the King above all gods. Come and worship Me, My child. Bow down before Me, because I am your God and I want a close relationship with you.[16]

Worship Me in the Spirit, rejoice in Christ Jesus, and have no confidence in the flesh.[17] As you worship Me and do My will, I promise I will hear your prayers.[18]

Always pursue what is good for yourself and others. Worship is always good for you; therefore, rejoice always, pray without ceasing, and in everything give thanks, for this is My will in Christ Jesus concerning you.[19]

As the God of peace, it is My will to sanctify you completely, that your whole spirit, soul, and body will be preserved blameless at the coming of your Lord Jesus

Christ. I have called you, and I am faithful to do all that I have promised to you.[20]

Worship Me, My child, and call to Me. I will answer you and show you great and mighty things, which you do not know.[21] I love you and I want you to spend time with Me. I receive your worship and your love.

With grace and blessing,

Your loving Father

References: *(1) John 4:23-24; (2) 1 John 1:3; (3) Psalms 16:11; (4) Matthew 4:10; (5) Jeremiah 31:3; (6) James 4:8; (7) Jeremiah 29:11-13; (8) Deuteronomy 6:5; (9) Deuteronomy 11:13; (10) Psalms 95:6; (11) Psalms 100; (12) Psalms 96:9; (13) Psalms 96:6; (14) Psalms 105:1-4; (15) Psalms 105:5; (16) Psalms 95:1-7; (17) Philippians 3:3; (18) John 9:31; (19) 1 Thessalonians 5:15-18; (20) 1 Thessalonians 5:23-24; (21) Jeremiah 33:3.*

Now you may wish to write a letter of personal response to God.